THE
#1
GUIDE
TO SAVE YOUR BUSINESS
FROM
LAZY
F@#KS!

TONY MARINO

THE #1 GUIDE TO SAVE YOUR BUSINESS FROM LAZY F@#KS!

First published 2021 by FIREDUPXO

Prepublication Data Service details available from the National Library of Australia.

ISBN: 978-0-9945328-7-9 (eBook)
ISBN: 978-0-9945328-6-2 (paperback)

Cover by FIREDUPXO

Players by EmoticonsHD

Thank you to the FU Research Crew, you are amazing.

THE FU MENU

TO YOU, YES YOU!

You are the Boss.

You are the one in charge.

Always busy, busy, busy.

Just never enough time in the day to get things done.

Think everything is sweet at work.

Don't believe you have a problem.

Would instead not stir the status quo.

And some other excuses that could fill this page and then some.

So, let's cut to the chase.

Drop your guard for a minute.

Park any ego or belief that it's all good and pay attention to what lies herein.

It is a reference guide, a how-to with just enough content, served up, frank and direct so you can use it to suss out if all is that good at your workplace or its adults playing up like they are in kindergarten or much worse.

1

I'm just giving you some pointers, without any sugar-coating.

You be the judge.

Okay?

Good.

Let's go!

IMPORTANT DISCLAIMER

This disclaimer is to any reasonable person with common sense.

This is to filter out those who are all uppity and are sensitive to these words, so we can at least talk freely and openly and be unapologetically politically incorrect and just say it like it is.

So, if you don't understand any of this, then do not proceed forward. It's just not for you. Read a children's book instead.

The statements and opinions in the material contained in this guide are for general informational purposes only, and reasonable care and skill have been used to compile this guide's content.

However, we, (the author, publisher, and content provider) make no warranty as to the accuracy or completeness of any information in this guide and accept no responsibility or liability for any inaccuracy or errors and omissions, or consequential loss or damage, arising from loss of data or profits, or for any damage or injury to persons or property arising out of the accessing or use of any content, information, instructions, methods, or ideas contained in this guide.

Any reliance you place on such information is therefore strictly at your own doing, your own risk or reward. The consequences are yours alone.

So, if you are on the fence, thinking, um I'm not sure about this, then clear off. It really is not for you. Thank you.

If yes, that is understood and acknowledged, then let's get stuck into it.

FOREWORD & MOVE FORWARD

Hi. Hello. Welcome, and let's start with just a bit of an out-there introduction first. Just to give some reference as to what I am even doing here with this guide.

Over the past half a century, I have been negative and positive and a whole heck of good and bad places in-between. I've been to the dark side plenty of times, the brighter side a few and seemed to fall somewhere in the middle depending on what was going on at the time. I've learned my lesson. Shit, I do hope so. Yes, I've been nice and cheeky and naughty, and I know that karma does come back around and it bites hard, and yes it really does hurt.

We have all been there at some point. It's how we react to it that makes the difference.

I've tried to rebel enough times, to fight the universe, and bring all my martial art skills to bear, yet it is a master in kicking my ass. Let me tell you; the universe has body-slammed me, kicked me in the nuts several times that my voice went all high pitched, and a few right hooks to the gut too. It has served up its form of punishment to me as I thought at times, I was a good citizen of the world, clearly not true. I very likely deserved it all.

I've sure learned that lesson. Thanks, Universe. So, now I choose to do my thing and just power ahead. I try to do good more than bad these days and just live a somewhat humble life and leave some outbursts for the fun times.

That is a lot of work in the making to try and find that Zen balance. Can you relate?

I very much know that this life isn't a rehearsal. We all know this. Yeah, the cliché - life is short. It so goddamn is.

And I'll tell you something, lovely people, I'm already at the more than halfway point so I am full-on, balls to the wall, going hard out and yes, I have to pull my head in many a time. I know this.

If we haven't met before, I'm Tony Marino. Soon, Dr Tony Marino, thank you very much. Ha, I dream. And I'm the direct, unfiltered, unapologetically politically incorrect crazy mother something dude but with a soft-centred heart, most of the time. Yes, I know a few people who would be rolling their eyes right about now reading this, aye you know who.

The truth is, being strong is about taking no shit, get real laser-focused and be all inspiring to yourself and that FU isn't a bad statement when put in context. Like the subject matter and intent of this guide. I'll explain why and then we can get started.

Over the past 30 years, numerous scenarios have presented themselves, thousands of people have weighed in on the topic of conversation and the consensus of this living breathing Doctor of Psychology thesis of mine, in the making, has been...

There are a lot of lazy f@#ks out there. You see them everywhere. I'm not kidding! You know exactly what I mean.

But seriously it's one worse when they are part of your company.

And to top the worse level, even worser (yes, I know it's not a word), is if it is you.

That's a whole another level of oh shit moments, and we'll get to that soon enough.

Please park your ego, that high and almighty attitude, or princess pout for this one.

Let's just keep it real!

IT HAS TO BE SAID

When this guide was being loaded with content, the live case examples and research were so readily available because of the multitude of people I have encountered over the years who wanted to share their stories. It was evident that people fitted into individual profiles based on their behaviour, work ethic, personal and professional traits.

So, on that premise, and with a team of lovelies helping me with the research, the idea for this FU guide was born. However, what came to be the almighty realisation as more and more people were being profiled and lots of content was made available to me, was that I became very aware that I was indeed several of the profiles wrapped up in one that I so seemly wrote about.

It was not the epiphany moment or that it revealed itself to me in some halo, but instead it was an oh shit point in time when I looked closely and went holy heck, and a few more choice words I won't repeat here and I knew that if I were the Boss, during those times, that I would have fired me.

Yes, it's widespread. You're not alone. If you're like most bosses, you have an unproductive, time-wasting, revenue blocking, couldn't give a toss, don't even try and touch me employee, even worse if you have a few. Ouch.

Well, let's stop the madness right now and take control. No more lazy f@#ks allowed!

Take a new approach. Take a solid look at your work environment. Is it a place people would want to work there? Do you want to be there too? We'll discuss that in detail, so you can genuinely evaluate for yourself.

And through this journey of discovery, we will challenge you to take an even closer look at yourself. Are you leading the team, managing the workforce or don't even want to be a part of the delegating? Yes, we will provide some framework for you to review that with all honesty too. Bet it will be an eye-opener and maybe your saving grace too.

If you haven't got all uptight and realise you have work to do, the next most crucial part is, who is on your team? Why are they there? Do they add value or just burn right through it? Should they stay or be moved on?

That's where you really must take an active interest in who's who in your 'zoo' and make some tough but essential decisions that benefit your company, not appease to, or pander to those in your workforce that should be given a right royal rev up otherwise just move them on.

Yes, you will need to ensure you have top-notch legal counsel, experts in employment law to ensure you do everything by the book and so you don't come unstuck in the process.

It is time to get ...absolutely ...100% certifiably ...
FIREDUP

THE SHIT'S ABOUT TO GET REAL

An E _ G T _ V moment. Fill in the blank letters. Reclaim your warrior spirit.

Take the whole god damn cake and eat it too.

Seriously, Fired Up is all about taking charge, taking the bull by its horns, and just getting things done.

Yes, that's right. It's time to reclaim authority, productivity, and work ethic. Roll them sleeves up; it's not going to be a walk in the park.

Let's run through how your company stacks up and then identify the profile and behaviours of each person in your team. Then we will discuss how you either make a judgement call to invest in them to pull these people into line, or you move them on.

It's not going to be pretty. You will need your game face on for this one. You are going to be called every name under the sun. You will be seen as a mean you know what.

But harden up otherwise your business will suffer because of toxic staff. It may very well already be. Time to eradicate it before your business turns to shit if it hasn't already.

Each weekday I see people, you see people, we all see people, certain people that can be best described as lazy f@#ks. You know exactly the ones I mean. Don't shake your head. You damn well know exactly what I'm referring to.

10

The ones, yes, those ones that front up right on start time, but rather than be productive and go straight to work, they decide now is the time to chat to people like they haven't seen them for years, make a coffee and even their breakfast. Monday's are the worst day for this.

Talk about taking the piss. Seriously they can get their ass out of bed earlier and have breakfast before work. They get a break or two during the day, so how about they be productive first aye.

When they arrive to work, for which we are giving them a decent day's pay (you better be), then we expect, in return, they give us their full attention and a decent workday. There is nothing unfair or mean about it; it's just what they need to do and which they would have damn well promoted how good, and productive they will be in the 'dress up, on good behaviour, best foot forward, please hire me' interview. Ugh, please! So quickly forgotten.

Furthermore, it does not take 15 minutes "oh just waiting for my computer to start up" bullshit! or "just have a lot of admin to catch up on before I make those calls Boss" more bullshit!

Seriously they need to front up otherwise if I had half the chance, I would say FU to them, and then F OFF and show them the door. It's happened to me and many others who have told their story, so we know it's not make-believe and as you read further, you too will be able to relate either way. It is the relatability that will help you sort your shit out and that of your employees who are taking a free ride.

I don't like passengers at work, and too many companies these days tolerate passengers. If you are the poor bastard who has a team like that or a couple of fly below the radar lazy ass types, we will definitely look at how we can deal with it.

We'll go from Angel to Devil as we look at each of the dozen profiles. It's time to regain some sense of workmanship from people and pay them well for their great productivity not just to prove that their ass can sit on a chair using your computer and hogging bandwidth all the while organising their holiday or consuming social media. At the same time, on the clock, that's your time.

If you like that sort of workplace abuse or just don't give a f@#k then stop reading and regift this guide to someone with some sense and FU. Otherwise, if you are ready to deal with this shit then read on and front up, and you might just regain some nirvana moments. At the very least, a productive work environment with respect for leadership might just be a great place to build the team.

I've decided to break down and focus in on each of the dozen 'players' so you can evaluate, honestly self-assess, where you sit now and if you want to do something about it or dial things up and take that journey from Angel to Devil if you dare.

It will be an interesting one but a fulfilling one if you successfully reclaim some sense of work ethic from those who should be thankful you've let them work for you.

You want them to be working hard not hardly working, which all too often it's the latter that is evident. Do something about it!

So, let's get into it.

A WAKE-UP CALL - READER BEWARE

I see you. You're a successful business owner. Your business has grown fast, and you now have more employees working in it than you ever believed possible. You're the Boss, the Coach of the Team but these days it feels more like the sin bin bench full of head cases and nut jobs! Your business ran much more smoothly when it was just you and your buddies, making it happen, right?

Well guess what?

Playtime is over. You're the Coach of the Team (remember?) and the reason your players are out of control? Yes, the Coach - You! And what are you doing about it? Sweet. F. All.

What you should be doing is getting Fired Up! It's easy to say, 'it's too hard' or 'I don't like to fire people'. It's also a cop-out. You're feeling a bit sorry for yourself because you 'didn't get into business to manage people'. You also didn't get into business to fail, either. Ultimately, fail is what your business will do if you don't get your shit together and manage your employees properly. If you can't handle it, then get someone who is a master at it.

A word of warning before you continue. I'm not here to sugar coat it for you. As the most important person at work, you're probably used to a little sugar with your shit. But I'm all about the unadulterated kind. The situation is not sweet, and it's not pretty either, and I won't pretend it is (that's what got you here in the first f@#king place!).

I'll also get in your face about your behaviours and attitudes. Frankly, it's your fault for sitting idle. Whether you want to believe it or not, you're to cop it for any people issues in your business. Even if you're a good leader in other areas, and you treat your staff well, if there are shitty people in your business, dragging things down, then you're guilty of one of the worst leadership mistakes. Inaction. She'll be right. Turn a blind eye. Sweep it under the rug.

It's not all doom and gloom though if you do something. There are few situations that aren't fixable but still, there is a way out for you. Some might get dirty before they're cleaned up properly. But it will definitely be worthwhile.

Enough small talk. It's time to FU.

THIS PAGE IS LEFT INTENTIONALLY BLANK

Why?

So that you can relax and get ready for that real awakening!

IS THIS REASONABLE?

Is it reasonable to expect that you have a business that your goal is to be successful, make a difference, grow revenue, achieve accolades, achieve your own goals etc.?

To help achieve that you need to build a team of highly productive, skilled, energetic, enthusiastic, team players who contribute, want to work to help achieve the business's outcomes and in return receive a good day's pay for a good days output?

Why then do companies have to be the obligatory stopgap for lazy people who just should not be in that line of work whatsoever and become an added burden to what pressures already exist in running a company? Why should you have to be the unlucky chosen one? Don't be!

Ensure you have excellent counsel in terms of a robust well-versed HR or Legal team who unequivocally have got your back. However, if the lazy ones exist in this team, let's put it politely - you are double f@#ked.

That's when devil mode incorporates special forces black ops, and you seek external counsel with those who are expert at employment law. This one will test your stamina and willpower, so ensure you plan accordingly, so you don't become undone in the process.

THE CULTURE SHINES BRIGHTLY

This is really important. I mean really important. Your organisation's culture is either positive or negative, motivating or demoralising, encouraging, wanting to be there, not dreary, a combat situation, or finding an excuse not to show up to work today type culture.

The culture starts at the top, absolutely, and it permeates through each department, area of work, touching all staff levels.

When the culture is all in the positive then production soars, pride in one's work is evident, good things happen, sales are made, revenue is rising, and people feed off it like it is a winning game.

How does the culture in your organisation stack up?

Be real. Is it great? Just okay? Or an absolute shithole?

We'll run you through the Corporate Engine Optimiser challenge shortly and provoke you with questions covering your areas of Service, Sales, Numbers, Leadership, Strategy and of course Personnel. You can honestly assess if you have all bases covered for what is a Good, Positive, Great, Encouraging, and Motivating place for you and your employees to thrive or whether you have work to do in certain areas to ensure that it is not Bad, Negative, Doom, Gloom, Sad, Depressing, and a Combat Zone.

It is designed to check if you have the 'house in order' or in other words, how does the company look, operate, stack up on a number of levels, including is it a place that would attract, motivate, keep, and empower its staff, team, employees, contributors to the bottom line?

Best we check on all of that first, then we will absolutely dive into the team to understand those who are keepers and those players who need to be moved on.

Be open-minded.

Be honest with your assessment.

Be prepared to make the changes necessary to create a harmonious, productive place without the crap and the lazy ass employees dragging the place down.

YOUR MANAGEMENT STYLE

Management style is a mixed bag. You have leaders who are in the right role and carry outstanding leadership traits, and some examples are Influencer, Innovator, Open and Honest, Good Listener, Great Communicator, Visionary, Decision Maker, Confident, Fair and Empathetic with others. There is, of course, much more to add.

Then you have those in a leadership position that would not even know how to organise a booze-up in a brewery, let alone command a team, manage direct reports, or others to supervise with any meaningful level of command presence.

I'm not talking about Sergeant Major in the Army, who first and foremost is a hard bastard, expertly designed to give lots of orders and crap and not liked one bit by his new recruits. In fact, in most armed forces, law enforcement and the like it is just a top-down kick-ass dictated approach that is a given and factored in by anyone who signs up and goes through the training and the ranks.

I'm specifically zooming in on the corporate world, small business, mom & pop operations and how the CEO, the Boss, the Managing Director, the top of the tree operates.

There is the top-down management style - direct, command, delegate, and then there is the flat structure management style - do as I say, let's work alongside each other. Which one are you?

THE COMPANY CHECKUP

Before we get into the nitty-gritty and the downright deep dive of who's who in your workplace, let's first of all just run a few checks so you can determine, with some honesty, that it is not a shit zone but a good work environment to attract and maintain good employees.

Let's run through the C.E.O, that is the Corporate Engine Optimiser and take a good look for yourself at the company, it's foundations, it's guiding principles, it's mission, it's modus operandi to see if they are all in check.

It will reveal any areas (outside of employees as we will get to that soon enough) that require attention, that's in need of an urgent fixer upper.

So, let's go from bottom to top and back again, cover all bases and as you read through the checklist be absolutely open with the answers. If you believe it does not correlate with your business, then move on with the next, but don't dismiss it or sugar-coat things and say no everything is alright. If it hits a nerve and you are not sure, or it is a sore point, then actually create a task to take a good look at it. It may just provide a better outcome.

The purpose of evaluating your business engine room is to ensure that the main areas are optimised, worked on, addressed, and noticed. You then know that what comes next will be an eye-opener and by that I mean, we will look at the dozen player profiles.

Any Boss or person in management overseeing a team must be of the right stuff otherwise its worse than the blind leading the blind, it's just downright bloody stupid!

BUILD A STRONG FOUNDATION.

CEO - CORPORATE ENGINE OPTIMISER™

FOR THE BOSS, CEO, CFO, CIO, CTO, THE BOARD, DIRECTOR, SENIOR EXECUTIVES, MANAGERS AND OTHERS IN LEADERSHIP.

How is your company doing?

We're not just talking about the P&L, what the bean counters are telling you or your staff are saying what they think you want to hear, but from your observations as Chief of the company, the Boss, and all its operations, how is it really doing?

This is a good starting point to get a good read on various critical areas of the company and your leadership style.

Not only is it a good corporate review, but also an excellent reality check for you as well. You will quickly be able to see what's on track and what needs review, correction and action.

You'll be able to task and hold those accountable, including yourself, who should have the company's best interests in mind, so it runs as smoothly and efficiently as possible.

And if you haven't been receiving good honest, accurate intel, then call those people into line and question them immediately. You must know what is happening in all areas while entrusting and empowering (not micromanaging) staff to lead and manage teams for you.

Time to get started. Read each checklist item in each section. Take your time. Reread it. Do not dismiss it unless it has no bearing on your business. We doubt many will be bypassed as we have researched hundreds of company operations, spoken with corporate movers and shakers and top business coaches to formulate this and make it as useful as possible to you.

Where the answer is not clear then task those items of key team members to investigate and report back to you directly, no sugar coating it, no fluff on top, no smoke and mirrors either. Just the facts so you can adequately assess. You should darn well know this.

CEO - CORPORATE ENGINE OPTIMISER™

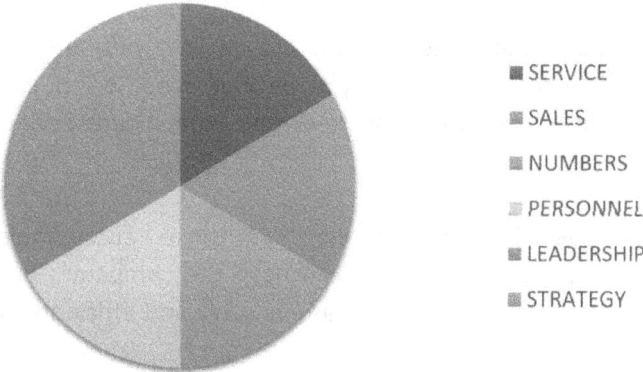

- SERVICE
- SALES
- NUMBERS
- PERSONNEL
- LEADERSHIP
- STRATEGY

THE SERVICE LEVEL

- The company has a system to quantitatively measure customer satisfaction, such as surveys, reviews, net promoter scores etc., and you are familiar with how the feedback and consensus are from your client base.
- Service standards are written, and staff are thoroughly aware of them, and it is another key metric for which company performance can be measured.
- TQM (Total Quality Management) program is in place and forms the basis or framework for quality assurance and a high level of sales, service, support, etc.
- New ideas for value improvement to products and services, to remain leading edge or to add another level of customer delight where possible is championed.
- Service or support is actioned and completed in a very prompt and timely manner. Where specific timeframes are communicated to the customer, these times are exceeded beyond expectations, where often possible. Going above and beyond.
- The company is well known for delivering the best service and the feedback, testimonials and reviews are evidence of this and shared with staff and customers.
- By knowing their customer, the company looks at ways to understand what their customers want before they know they do. Continuous surprise and delight keep them loyal to the company service offering.
- There is a solid leadership structure for day-to-day operating decisions.
- The staff takes pride in their work, producing high quality, accurate, professional output with no cowboy approach or cutting corners.

- The team is highly productive, and there is no unnecessary double up or do-over of their work output.
- Everyone knows their place, position and the work decisions that need to be made to perform at a top-level and no sub-par is allowed.
- Every review, team huddle or meeting accomplishes specific, measurable, actionable outcomes and not a meeting to have a meeting to organise the next meeting.
- Operating principles, customer ethos of your organisation is known, practised, and routinely reviewed and enhanced.
- The team is aware of every mistake or reason for a client or customer account loss, and this is discussed to look for improvement or to handle at a high-quality level.
- Open door policy enables the team to champion areas of improvement, ideas, or suggestions to make the workplace, service, or product better, and everyone is encouraged to participate.
- The staff has the necessary training, skills, know-how, and specific equipment to do their work and enhance it to the next level of productivity or output.
- A streamlined process of order fulfilment or document control exists so that there are minimal touchpoints from order to delivery or at least a strong record-keeping system to provide in-depth business analysis reporting to view each area.
- In this day and age, the company's operations are computerised, automated, cloud-based, shared with authorised staff at various levels for management, oversight, etc.

- Very few issues occur in any one area of the company, and if they do, it is immediately addressed and rectified, so there is little to no downtime and as an error-free operation is maintained where possible.
- Regular review meetings with key clientele are held to discuss the service level they receive, looking for ways to improve, and ultimately offer more of your offering if applicable and in-turn that feedback is evaluated and used to improve those areas that can enhance the business.

THE SALES SUPERSTARS

- Sales are being handled by those who can sell. No extra passengers in the sales department are allowed. Great time to watch the Glengarry Glen Ross video clip with Alec Baldwin from 1992 (search online). It's an oldie, but a goodie of just how much dead weight some sales organisations carry. Colourful language from Alec as well, anyway, take a pause, have a giggle, see what you draw from it and if any crazy semblance to your operation or a heck no and be thankful you have something way better, and the sales team are converting, not moaning about no golden leads.
- Salespeople are managed daily, and a weekly wrap-up of results and great achievement is well-touted while those with sub-par results are known and helped up or out.
- Every salesperson has KPIs and targets set, and they are highly motivated to meet those daily, weekly, monthly quotas.
- The sales team are motivated, productive, and there is high morale, and they are successful.
- Sales targets, team-based, and individual results are displayed on a leader board for all to see.
- The remuneration structure, whether commission, bonus or performance pay is rewarding, motivating and provides an incentive that is achievable with great conversions, not a dangling sales carrot that is unattainable and negatively affects the output.
- The sales team also has a collective team goal, so all have the opportunity to benefit from each other's strengths and teamwork in a collaborative way for the company, and a team reward is given when they blast right through it.

- Sales output is on the increase, whether it's more volume, larger orders, repeat sales, or referral business etc.
- Sales Leadership monitor sales performance and output against target projections and ensure timely communication to the team, so all in the know are well aware of how sales are trending and where possible real-time reporting and communication is happening.
- Where applicable, there is a high turnover of product, widget, service offerings to drive revenue for the company.
- Customer referrals, repeat purchases, and high satisfaction is measurably trending positively.
- Other departments provide great support to the sales staff, and everyone encourages each other as part of the broader organisation from management, administration, sales, marketing, operations, delivery, and service, etc.
- Sales team attracts high performing individuals, and there is less than 15-20% turnover of salespeople annually.

THE NUMBERS GAME

- The numbers are accurate, systemised, and real-time reporting is available and monitored.
- All income is received on schedule, and no favours or deals extended for late payments with customers unless final management approval for such exceptions (not the rule) is authorised.
- All obligations that are due and payable are handled on time, and no one is chasing the company for payments.
- Staff payroll is automated, trackable, accurate and systemised for ease of processing and can be reported on at any time.
- General and Administrative (G&A) expenditure is kept closely in check and on a downward trend compared as a percentage of the net, not gross sales.
- Inventory count, stock taking, and accurate processes are in place to ensure up-to-date inventory reconciliation and reporting.
- Accounts payable is current, and all invoices and/or purchase orders to be dealt with are taken care of.
- Financial statements are always completed on time.
- Reporting is provided to all department heads to assist with their management of each area, and so everyone in the know has the transparency needed to be effective in their leadership and oversight and ultimately, production output.
- The ratio of total debt to equity for the company decreased last year, and the debt service as a percentage of gross profit also declined.
- Accounts receivable is efficiently managed and received in a timely and acceptable period per sales/service agreements.

- Loan payments are current, and all agreement terms are being met.
- Finance/Accounting department is expertly and efficiently operating and always looking at ways to be cost-effective.
- Profit margins have increased for sales, service, or products over the last 2-3 years.
- There is a detailed budget and forecast that management and those within the Finance/Accounting department routinely review and discuss from a high-level operational standpoint so that good company decisions can be made.
- The company's break-even ratio is low, and profitability is very good, and it is profit-focused not just a revenue-based operation.
- Where the company is dependent on the sales, service or product offering, there is a continuous supply of sales via repeat or ongoing service than just a one-pop offering, unless such one-time sales can garner referral business that converts.
- Not one specific client accounts for more than 20-25% of the total sales or receivables where you rely too heavily on one entity to run the company or for unforeseen circumstances, ruin it if they were to move to a competitor tomorrow.

THE PERSONNEL PLAYBOOK

- Staff accountabilities are written and straightforward. Not just a job description referenced in one's employment contract and never looked at again, but actual job duties and responsibilities and KPIs and performance expectations etc. are stated and known and acknowledged by each employee and conveyed in regular performance reviews.
- Each staff member knows what their contribution is. This is spelled out very clearly. They know exactly how the business operates, how it is profitable, and in-turn each staff member knows precisely what is required and expected of them.
- Every manager is a positive reflection of the company core values and is highly qualified, trained, certified, experienced, educated, positive, motivated, efficient, productive and loyal contributor. Woo, that would be a nice place to be right? Make it happen.
- At a minimum, there are quarterly employee reviews conducted. They are not rescheduled last minute because it's too busy, or we promise to get to that shortly, but actually, a meeting is conducted, and several key areas are reviewed, and any praise is given, corrective action is taken, and performance discussed as well as next steps, training gaps, certification, upskill, and so forth.
- Team members are well aware of the chain of command for reporting to and following instructions of and there is no dual chain of command or conflicting directives from leadership.

- Each employee is in a job that uses their strengths; there is no suffering or mismatches. This is a vital area that must be reviewed, not just in conjunction with who is in the right role and at the highest and most optimal use. And that the opposite is not true, and the employee is absolutely the wrong fit for the role, possibly has strengths in another area that could enhance the operation as well as boost their morale, or in fact, could just be the wrong fit for the company altogether and it's time for them to go.

- Every employee is trained, highly competent and skilled and provided the necessary tools to perform their role. There are no weak links or passengers on board, or any toxic behaviour tolerated; otherwise, it is immediately handled.

- No staff member is cruising, non-performing, lazy, or propped up by others, so no passengers are allowed, only productive team players and contributors exist.

- Expectations are clear, timelines set, deadlines kept, production quota met, and all team members are in sync with this.

- The company provides a great place to work and be rewarded, and staff want to be there, contribute and feel part of a successful team without any drama.

- Consequences are imposed for non-performance. This discussion addresses non-performance, issue warning, and corrective action as necessary and important to closely monitor this. Suppose the employee has redeemable qualities and the time is spent to assist or accommodate within reason. In that case, it may just be a bump in the road, and things correct themselves for the better, and you are a positive part of that, and the company wins too. Or suppose there is just no interest in taking ownership and accepting one's non-performance or a complete lack of respect for the workplace etc. In that case, this is another reason to go bye-bye and not delay the exit either.

THE LEADERSHIP, THE CEO, THE BOSS

- CEO has a very strong vision and desired outcome for the company, and it is communicated to all staff, and there is clear direction forward. No fumbling about.
- The company has a clear and concise mission statement. Its modus operandi is not pie in the sky but real, doable, and the team believes in it, and the CEO demonstrates it.
- The company's culture is positive, encouraging, motivating and not at all combative, toxic, or demoralising, and the Boss is a positive example to all.
- Boss is a true leader and helps others become leaders, not just managers.
- The Boss frequently interacts with the team across all departments and not stationed in the office all the time or never visits other locations whether physically or virtually and ensures that they remain connected with the team and keep spirits high.
- CEO sets big goals and targets for the company and encourages all to help achieve them.
- CEO often acknowledges, praises, calls out great achievements and contributions from staff and keeps team morale high.
- CEO has enough time to continue with the vision and to drive the company forward and has a highly efficient and professional team who handles operational minutia effectively, so there is space to move, and they are not putting out little fires every minute of the day and taking their eyes off the prize.
- CEO is beyond excited with stellar company results, and such attitude is expressed positively and permeates through the company when success is on a high.

- Boss is positive, encouraging, and maintains a good life outside of work and so there is that work/life balance and not all consumed work pressures around the clock that then affects the work environment if personal baggage is dumped at work.
- Boss has an excellent professional work ethic, communicative with all workforce levels, is respected and gives respect to others.
- CEO is a nice person, yet firm and fair in their approach to running a busy, productive company that is out to positively smash its goals and be profitable and successful.

THE STRATEGIC DIRECTION

- The company has a business plan that sets forth the strategic and operational objectives and programs for the year, and this is communicated across the various departments for all those in the know, and it is monitored regularly.
- The company's product, widget or service is either a necessity, highly sought after or of great quality to serve up.
- Regular strategy meetings are held with the team to ensure operationally and tactically everyone knows what is expected, and is highly productive following the company mission, directive, and targets.
- In conjunction with senior leadership, the management team ensures all targets, and sales forecasts are managed expertly to ensure efficient staffing levels, inventory, marketing, and sales drive to the marketplace.
- The company business plan and targets provide a clear direction for all team to support that outcome and align with the mission statement. There is no mismatch.
- The company has partnered with the best professional resources such as accountants, lawyers, trainers, consultants, marketing agencies, recruiters, manufacturers, etc. that compliment their business and provide significant support and service as required and are reviewed regularly to ensure they are providing the best outcomes.
- The company has multiple suppliers or resource options and not reliant on a single entity, whether domestically or internationally based and has options available to them.
- The company has standing in the marketplace, is well-known or a top provider within their sector, industry, service or offering.

- The company's sales or service offering is competitively priced and not a discounting volume play business yet has good profit margins on the product, and the marketplace perceives great value for such pricing.
- The company has ample resources in motivated, highly trained staff, great marketing, top product or service, sufficient cash or finance resources, ample inventory to handle it's short to mid-term goals.

THOUGHT-PROVOKING LINE
OF QUESTIONING

- Your Product or Service is inexpensive, or you have low margins and just push volume and fingers crossed, see if it adds up at the end of the month.
- Opportunities for repeat or add-on sales are limited, or a solution has never been implemented to open a new channel, including referrals, affiliates, reward-based etc.
- There is no involvement with industry events, tradeshows, online and offline advertising and publications etc. that showcase, highlight, advertise or pitch your product, service, or business.
- Your ability to conduct a thorough business intelligence or sales report on any customer/client to assist with upsells, service reviews, marketing campaigns etc. is inadequate and spread across paper reports, database, CRM and is all over the show.
- The purchase is not a high priority for your customer, or your marketing has not pushed that to front and centre of their decision buying process and create any sense of urgency or leading-edge reason as to why they should act now.
- Prospects and customers/clients are not exposed easily to your business online, via persistently targeted marketing campaigns or readily aware of your products, services, or business offering.
- There are no new channels opened to move your product or service and continues to be the same way different day nothing new opening up new avenues to the marketplace.
- The sales cycle is a long process and requires lots of handholding, yet no real concierge or multi-touchpoint

premier program is offered and monitored and evaluated as to whether there are areas that might be enhanced that could improve the length of the sales process without cutting any great customer service corners.

- There is no partnership or association, or community connection known to your prospects or customers/clients that provides another awareness point for your company.
- There are competitors within your market/sector that appear just to do things so much better, yet your competitive intelligence is non-existent to understand what market attack points you could zoom in on to potentially capture more market share then you have seen before.
- Your business has a complicated product or service that is not understood, and the efforts to provide education to help with sales conversions are non-existent.
- Need to establish a new brand, product, or service against the established competition, yet no discovery has been made or researched as to its viability to open a new channel or sales/service line. You have not even asked your team for ideas.

THROW IN A TEAM CHALLENGE

Okay all done? Are there some eye-openers at all? Of course, there were. Some certainly you would gloss over as it may not relate to you or you cannot relate to it and thus rule it out; however, many can help thought provoke as to whether you provide a good workplace, with amenities, training, support, teamwork, reward, recognition, management, right attitude, great aptitude, professionalism, skills, history, and solid mission statement and be damn well proud of it.

So, review the list again, now with key staff and fix and refine areas that could make it even better. No one wants to work for a company that treats their people like shit as well as the workplace is the same. If you are not sure, stop and put all ego and guesswork aside and run an anonymous survey and see for yourself.

If you don't already solicit feedback, have open communication lines and champion ideas and suggestions, how the hell do you know how you are doing? Come on get it together.

Think about the talent you have within and another good way to see who is on board and engaged with the company and who is just going with the flow or seriously cruising, and you have done nothing about it.

With all the evaluation of whether your company is reaching for the stars and not stuck in, you know what and to check the level of employee engagement, consider a Think Tank Challenge competition and solicit great ideas from within the organisation. Yes, of course, give away some cool prizes (possibly consider time off which is valuable to many these days) and even have winners selected based on peer review and scoring, so the team is involved.

This is another way to build productivity, boost team morale, power up those employees who are real team players and reveal those who may just not be keen at all to be involved.

Just another way to review who you have helping towards the company mission and not hindering it.

Some ideas for the competition are:

- Build a plan that helps develop a sense of urgency, a reliance on, a better value proposition, and to attract customers to do business with the company.
- Develop a brand new channel to deliver your product/ service.
- Design a new product offering that may bundle or package several products and/or services into either a recurring subscription type model or an offering at a premium price.
- Initiate a reward or VIP service, an alliance or referral network, or partnership to access more business with potentially pre-qualified customers.
- Create an attention-grabbing marketing campaign to stand out from the competitors and showcase the company products or service to capture more prospects, better than any Agency has done before.
- Create an educational offering, or classes or mentoring platform to help educate and ultimately empower

the end-user or client of your product or service and whether those classes are held locally, virtually, offer certification, or overall improve the client satisfaction and adoption and usage of the product or service.

This is mentioned as a great team-building exercise for the company. A great way to tap into the skills, knowledge, ideas others may have brought over with them from other employers (possibly competitors) for which they never had the opportunity to champion.

And of course, it is another measurement as to who the contributors are, team players and detractors within the organisation and if you did not already know, then this is an excellent way to double-check your intuition and suspicion.

At the very best, some new ideas come forward and can help with more momentum positively for the business and all because you took the initiative.

And there is no downside to this exercise as those who in any way are negative to the idea may just be highlighting to you the need for them to be moved on. That is a good thing. No passengers, no lazy f@#ks allowed.

WHAT'S YOUR COMPANY CORE VALUES?

Do you have them? Are they known throughout the company? Are they really at the core of what you do? Could your employees recite them, if quizzed? What about you? Check out this cool Monster Insights company core values with a twist I added. How good is yours?

We are always reminded that anywhere, anytime, whether we are working or playing in public or private, we strive to follow our core values:

People - We treat our team like family and our clients as our #1 priority. We put people first.

Passion - We love what we do and do what we love.

Product - We do not just build blah. We make the best and are committed to our pursuit of perfection.

Process - We work hard so we can play hard. We work very smartly too. We create a playing field that allows everyone to have their best game, be accountable and nicely rewarded.

Profit - We are a for-profit company, 100% and we are all about growth and profit, so we are then able to sustain our aggressive plans to build and control our destiny and pay it forward.

Philanthropy - We are a giving and supporting team who help as much as we can to make this world a better place and leave a legacy for future generations.

Pride - We take great pride in meeting new people from all walks of life, across the globe and whether we engage with them for a reason or for just a season, we appreciate knowing them. Maybe we get to meet you.

PICK ME PICK ME

Make sure you hire the right person who best fits your organisation. Easier said than done, right? How many times have you stuffed that one up or actually got it right?

Yes, sometimes it is a lucky dip or guesswork until you see one's productiveness, performance, teamwork and more and how that is sustained over some time, whereas others you can just gauge right away that it's a no go and deal with it while that probationary period is applicable and time to say bye-bye.

It is a delicate balancing act so you must be thorough and as indicated by research and discussing with recruitment companies who are honest to share their success rate, is that if you get it wrong and then need to rehire for the role, it can cost on average 25% to 150% of that original employee's annual salary. That is a whole helluva lot of money, money that could be used in other more productive ways for the business. Keep this in mind as we talk about removing non-performing employees, as this puts it in perspective, the costs associated with hiring, getting it wrong, then exiting and starting over. We'll help a little with that herein.

Lots of resumes and CV's prove that black ink sticks to white paper (if you print the pages that is), where the meaning of this snarky comment is that the content is so subjective, numbers quoted, projects completed, skillset attained, accolades and more can be the truth, half-truth or nothing resembling the truth and just added in for oomph.

It is an opportunity to embellish and pique the hiring person's interest as the competition in the submission process, let alone to get an interview is tough.

Creative, cheeky, and clever are all tactics required to get noticed to be put in the callback pile, hopefully, to get a call, even to get an interview. That's just the beginning. Oh boy.

Pre-Screening

Why them? Hundreds of applicants, no time to screen them, decide who is advanced to the next stage, or are eliminated?

Those applying for a role are an actor/actress vying for the Hire Me Oscar night award. Their audition, well for the most part, virtually at this stage, is to try and stand out, catch the eye, use the right kick-ass words on their resume to get a look in. You can't blame them for trying.

Then, if they can get in front of you, they are on their best behaviour, ready to pitch like Donkey from Shrek, "pick me, pick me". It's understandable. The competition is fierce, and for many roles, it is plentiful in terms of candidates. It's not an easy gig by any means to apply for a position, let alone have no idea where they even place, if they will get a callback or better yet, an interview.

Sure, suppose you have the dollars to invest in a recruitment company to do the heavy lifting for you. In that case, this can be one of the best routes to take if you are time-poor, hiring is not your forte, the role is specialised, or a specific set of skills is sought after.

Not only do recruiters have potential candidates in their database or know all the avenues to source prospects, but some also have some mad skills in helping you headhunt from the competition if the price is right in terms of what you are offering.

It's a good avenue to explore and expect to part with a reasonable fee for successful placement. Some agencies even offer a rehire service if for any reason they get it wrong, maybe the new hire did such a good actor stitch-up job on the interview to find out they are useless for the role, that they will seek to replace that person. So worth looking to see if they have this option or how successful they are in placing their first selection for the role. Ask them straight up to tell you.

If you have to do it all yourself and the hiring budget is tight, then some great pre-screening options are to run people through a discovery process before deciding if you want to interview them and take up even more of your valuable, never get it back, time.

Many of these things can be automated where people need to go on camera and explain a little more about who they are, introduce themselves and why they feel they are perfect for the role.

It's a good time to get some response back from them, so you know for real if that person that you're discussing this role with, gives off a good first impression and not be contradictory to their resume and cover letter, and you go huh, is this even the same person.

In terms of discovery or pre-screening, have them complete some aptitude tests, psychometric assessments like HBDI profiles, DISC, behavioural personality tests, albeit there is a cost, so long as you see this as an investment which it definitely is. The expense of removing them if you get it wrong is a lot more expensive, way more work, and just a negative place to end up.

If you're looking for a key employee and not just going on a gut feel and potentially get hit with the crap, later on, this type of testing can help you screen, and ultimately you can use more of these to try and refine the shortlist of candidates that you go okay this has a propensity to work out quite well, so I'm going to get them in for an interview.

To suss them out a little bit more, you might get them to do some homework like an essay or state a scenario and ask them to expand upon it to answer some key questions related to the role.

These people who are keen and are not the ones just doing a mass apply of every job there is out there will take the time to do it because someone is potentially interested in them rather than just stacking up on the desk or just cluttering up that inbox and you're never going to get to it. Now they feel a little bit of love along the way; whether or not they even get in front of you to interview, to get an offer, they will try their best to impress you.

So, the pre-screening is essential, and that's why sometimes a recruiter or agency is very useful because they do all the groundwork for you thoroughly.

Furthermore, they'll go ahead and shortlist candidates and do the initial interview process for you and then give you a summation of the candidates and their reasons or rationale behind why they are pitching these people to you.

Ultimately, yes, their job is to find someone for you that's a suitable candidate, not just matches the skill set you require, yet turns out to be a great employee, and of course, that's how they make their money, and they rightly deserve it.

Psychometric, Aptitude or Behavioural Profiling Testing

Psychometric assessments are highly recommended as an excellent tool to identify top performers as the testing can be customised, zoom in on a particular role and what requirements, skills, behavioural traits and so forth comprise the assessment.

Because of the large volume of assessments conducted, the peer group statistics and data amassed give some excellent intel and insight into enabling employers to make better-informed decisions about a candidate 'fit' for a particular role.

These assessments can increase the pre-screening stage, weeding out those who are unsuitable, zeroing in on those who deserve to advance to next phase of the selection process and enables one to learn more about how does this person think, solve problems, overcome challenges, leadership skills, personality, teamwork and much more.

The methodology and science behind these assessments can help select a candidate's suitability and their on-the-job performance. It's not foolproof, of course, but it is a potent and useful tool in the recruitment process. It is also valuable to have current employees complete one as part of a performance review to understand who's who in your 'zoo'. This is very valuable if you inherited a team, did not place specific individuals, or have any knowledge of who they are, their skills, experience, contribution to the company and so forth.

The benefit of conducting this pre-screening style is that it can uncover many areas that are not typically revealed during an interview.

The cost to deploy an assessment is well worth it and can save thousands of dollars in the long run if you have to exit the employee because they are useless, to put it bluntly. You know what I mean.

This is not a sole decision-making tool but an essential one that can help give a more comprehensive overview of one's suitability, strengths, character, areas of weakness and teamwork, to name just a few. The areas you can test for can be very broad or focused as required for the role you are hiring for. Any insight at this stage is a hell of a lot better than finding out on the job and it's too late.

Another benefit of assessing candidates is providing the same test. This sets up a fairer playing field. This way, you can review and compare answers from one candidate to another to help shortlist much faster.

This is an area that is highly recommended to help with your hiring process and get an early warning sign of a potential 'player' who you do not want on your team or have current staff complete it as part of a formal review. It is also useful for existing staff to identify training gaps, right person, right role, right time assessment and more. It can be a big wake-up call indeed and also can help pinpoint some of those flying under the radar types that you need to check up on a bit more or move on out.

It is also a great way to uncover other areas of skill, understanding, the experience that candidates or current staff may have that can assist with allocating the right role, promote to leadership roles or invest in special training and courses to team members, to not only show the company is focused on their people but to also look at ways to improve the culture and productivity and so much more.

References

Reference Checking - is more than just contacting the named referees as that is already a 'stitch-up' meaning they are only going to say good things that you want to hear anyway, rehearsed for the most part. Even contacting previous employers will likely validate the role and length of time employed if the employer even wants to provide that information. They are under no obligation to do so. And if they are courteous to serve up that limited information, it is complicated to glean any further intel (most employers will not divulge more anyway for privacy reasons).

Utterly understandable as I wouldn't say boo for the most part anyway, unless that ex-employee was a nice person, and had asked me to assist them, then I make an exception. Random, unexpected solicitation from a future employer for an ex-employee is not something I entertain. It only benefits one person, them and takes up your precious time.

Reference checking is a delicate one too because the people who provide you with their references have already given those people a heads up that you might get a call from so and so, and yes tell them I am great, yes, I can drive a forklift, I know how to build Excel macros and am a guru at PHP code, a master at graphic design and a talented machinist, blah blah.

Whatever it is, these references are only being given up as referees because they're going to say something nice. You cannot just call other employers that they've worked for, again for privacy. They will not reveal any personal information or work behaviour type of information unless they happen to be a chatterbox.

Sometimes you have to become a bit of a private detective, bit of a troll of sorts and check out online as it is one of the first places for many people who will spout where they've been on their LinkedIn profile and then look through various social media pages, to see what they have posted or even if they published articles, etc. That gives a bit of an insight into who they are and another side that you don't see in an interview obviously.

This can be another review process, better than reference checking that can add more value than the typical, traditional, going through the discovery motions. This can reveal some very interesting, complimentary, or downright oh hell no information. It's public so game on.

Suppose all you rely on for your pre-screening is reference checking than it's already pretty much saying hi, you have been nominated as a referee by Sarah. In that case, she's applying for a role with our company as a freight dispatcher, and I wanted to ask you a few questions. Yep, sure go ahead I have all the answers scripted anyway, as I thought you'd be calling me like Sarah said you might. You know it's really of little value, but I get it you are just going through the motions aren't you, so that you could say to somebody higher up in the company, yeah, I checked Sarah's references.

So, take what you get with little fanfare in terms of reference checking, yet dig deeper in terms of finding out more about these people online, through social media channels to find out more about their behaviour, character, to find out if they've written articles, what else they freely publicly display.

This can be invaluable information to help in yourdecision-making process.

Interview Process

Drop the bullshit questions that so many recruitment staff are told to say (and is so predictable) about how they are conducting the interview that it is easy to have all the answers. I am talking about long overdone questions like this classic one for example:

Q. Where do you see yourself in five years?
A. Hmmm, pregnant with my second child.
A. Doing your role as manager.
A. In Italy, once I earn enough to get there.

or

Tell me about a time where you had a challenging task to do, what was it, and how did you overcome it, meh, boring waste of time. Just an interviewer who is going through the motions.

Seriously, you know exactly what I mean by this. No one can predict with any certainty where they will be in 5 years, so it is a hypothetical question that carries no merit at all.

Instead of pretending, actually deal with a real scenario from your perspective within the workplace. Describe a situation that has happened for real, how would they handle it?

This way, their story is not made up and rehearsed, but on the spot to see how they respond. Maybe they draw a blank, are flustered, stumble or give it a good go at formulating a reply and this way you can assess on several levels.

ONBOARD FOR SUCCESS NOT A MESS

Onboarding begins immediately when you offer them a role and organise their start date. Now you're going to have the contract and employment agreement prepared. The terms will be spelled out very specifically of the role, the responsibilities, and the duties so there is no miscommunication from what was discussed.

You're also going to incorporate a probationary period so that you have a chance to exit them if things turn out that they are a lazy f@#k or worse.

This onboarding preparation, employment contract, etc., is an opportunity to restate what you said in their initial interview about what's required and expected from them.

Be sure to incorporate any KPI's and performance measurement criteria right from the get-go (yes it will change over time as your business evolves). In writing, you have some clear expectations, agreement from both parties and the groundwork is laid from the start.

Remember this employee is going to be obedient to the process at this stage because they are formalising an employment agreement with you and obviously want to work for you, so of course, they're going to say yes, so make sure that everything is spelled out professionally in the employment contract and that they are given a reasonable time to review it, ask questions if necessary, fully understand, agree, sign, and accept to join the team.

Then from that point forward, there needs to be a formal induction and onboarding process, not just let them rock up to work and show them around the office, where they can park their car, get set up with technology, meet the team, all of those typical types of niceties and then consider that is the extent of their onboarding and that's it. Do it properly.

Let's get the actual onboarding, training and induction process sorted, so you take them through training and mentoring from their direct report or a senior within the organisation to show them how to do things the way you want them to, hired them for and agreed contractually to do. On your part, anything less is a cop-out, and you will bear the brunt of this at a future point in time when it all turns to shit. Your fault.

Perhaps you have them sitting in front of a computer running through online tutorials, or a classroom-style format where there is a group of new employees starting simultaneously, buddying up with various employees to learn more hands-on about the role, or it may be some or all of the above. Yet it better not be, hey here are the keys for the forklift, go and retrieve those pallets of wine up in the racking system and load that truck over there, but hurry up please because the driver starts his delivery run in an hour. WTF. Don't you dare.

The duration of the onboarding process depends on the industry, the role, the requirements but must take time to ensure the onboarding, the training, the induction, and overall experience from day one is professional and thorough and not to just leave them to their own devices with the headset on and say OK go ahead and study this online course and I'll be back in three hours. Sadly, this type of onboarding exists, and it's a lazy employer approach, just going through the motions, and they are rolling the dice on how well things will turn out. Good luck with that.

Make it interesting, challenging, instructive and informative so when they finish, they have learned what is needed to perform the role, to be productive, efficient, understand the core competencies and confidence to show what they are capable of, to exceed their KPIs and not be a walking disaster, potentially creating some sort of workplace mess, health, or safety issues, etc. because your onboarding was absolute crap.

This is an investment in your people, in your team, so you don't become the lazy f@#k employer, then there is no hope for you.

Set Clear Expectations

Just to double back around for a minute concerning the employment contract which we know is going to be the first place of where you're going to formally scope out what the work responsibilities, the duties are and any KPIs or performance results that you want to have met or exceeded for the new employee.

And this may be subject to change, depending on various conditions that may arise, such as market or business conditions, etc. yet is imperative that this person puts their best foot forward, that you have told them how to take that step, in terms of what you need them to do, that it is thoroughly stated and clearly understood. That includes hours of work, production, reporting, dress code, perhaps a uniform, protective gear, etc.

Outline the time period required to get certifications, if they don't already hold them and the formal training that will be provided to them, the onboarding process, any assessments etc. along the way, including notice of regular performance reviews to be conducted.

In other words, if someone else in the company was to review an employee's role, responsibilities, and duties, could they articulate properly what is expected of that new employee?

Tell them what you are going to tell them. Tell them. Then tell them what you told them.

Clear? Good. If it's not, then tidy it up for Christ's sake pronto.

HOW DO THEY STACK UP?

How productive is your workforce?

Now you've gone through the Corporate Engine Optimiser checklists and analysed several areas from service to the numbers to productivity, to your team, you should now have a much better idea than just a gut feel. So really, how productive are the team?

This can help you look at the sales, revenue and profit and you can see if everyone contributed to that and you have a cohesive team or if there were a few stellar performers that got you across the line. Did some sales superstars score a few big sales and that happened to be your consensus of having a productive workforce when a few individuals happened to be the determining factor? Take a moment to consider how productive your workforce is and drill down to the individual employee to assess everyone's contribution.

Does each team member know what to do?

So, beyond what the role, responsibilities and duties were prescribed in the employment contract, and whether the employee is at day one, day fifty-two or could even be six months on, do they know what is required of them in the role? Do they know what to do each day when they show up to work? Of course, they do, right?

Like, here is the conveyor belt that we're running for the product line and the ultimate goal is to ensure that we push out 300 bottles of this every hour, then boxed, wrapped, palletised, loaded on the truck and delivered fresh within 24 hours to our customer from the time they ordered. For example, do your employees know what is expected and where their role and responsibility is in the 'chain' and how it affects the entire production not just have a micro-focused view of the operation? You best be double sure of this or get onto it right away.

Is there an overlap of workers' duties?

Is there an overlap of work duties, meaning is that purposeful and that you have almost a buddy system or if something happens someone is sick, on holiday or whatever happens that person can step in and perform the role?

Or are these people working beside each other performing very similar overlapped responsibilities because you need to increase output and that one person you would essentially believe could do it is just not up to speed or is it a requirement you have put in place as a business practice?

Whatever it is, it's a good opportunity to evaluate can one person at their top peak performance do this role? Yes or no, or no you need to have two people to be able to do it to buddy up to quality check, and you are okay that there is overlap as that is your insurance policy if someone leaves, is sick, on holiday or another scenario that leaves you exposed.

You will know the answer for this, yet it's just worth pausing and considering for a minute is an extra payroll required or can one top-notch employee do what you need to do? You decide and as you do, factor in if that employee currently in that role is at their peak performance, are they suited for the role, is too much workload placed on them, and you are rolling the dice for burnout, low morale etc. Yes, you have to evaluate all sides to this, so do it.

In all sincerity - are they well suited for the job?

And this one requires a little bit more thinking, and assessment truthfully are they suited for the job or are they a nephew of yours or your friend's cousin, and they just happen to get the role, or they've been there forever, and there is no effort to make a change. Or perhaps, you moved them around to do someone else's role because they left, and you didn't replace them, and you have just moved on and not paid any further attention.

Time to evaluate are they suited for the role? Are they in the right place, the highest use and perform or just a stopgap that you've not decided to take care of and replace with somebody competent and an outperformer in that role?

So, take the time to assess it and be honest about it, that there are no passengers allowed and you're driving a successful business so have drivers, not people who are in cruise mode because if they are, then you are guilty of sitting on your ass and allowing this to play out.

Are there particular ways of getting the job done?

Now I'm not talking about cutting corners here I'm asking a serious question, is there a specific method, process, or procedure for getting that particular job done?

There's so many industries, so many sectors, so many products and services that aren't just on a conveyor belt and there's a particular process of how you start the machine and load the product and go ahead and manufacture it, etc. which would therefore obviously answer that question. Yes, there is a particular way of getting the job done.

However, are there other ways of getting the job done where people could cut corners, not in an efficient manner but just cut corners to get the job done because they're bored and complacent and they wish to get through their day so they can say, yes Boss I've done those 300 bottles for you, all finished thank you, bye-bye.

And you think it's cool, not checking that no one's going to QA their work to find out it's subpar, it's crap actually, and it may very well be your customer who tells you, or you just lose future business with that client ever saying boo, and you will never know why.

So, is there a certain defined way of getting the job done? Is it documented, and have they been trained on it? Could they teach you, so you know what the retention is of their education, skill, and experience on this particular role?

Very few bosses have the time, the interest, the patience, and inquisitive nature to check their production line, whereas imagine how much would be learned if, for a few hours, completely unannounced the Boss said to Frank, I'd like to work alongside you for a while to see how this machine works and follow the process downstream to know whether we can increase further production. I am considering whether I go ahead and add another machine to the company or open another channel, perhaps another line of work. I want to see if there are any bottlenecks and ways you think we could improve it and get a bit more efficient, so if you don't mind, I'd like to observe and learn more how to make things better.

You get the idea. Have you done it? You will gather a lot of intel about the employee, the work environment, the process and more to help create the right corporate culture, that productive business and a place the team and you want to be a part of. Good things can come from this exercise, regardless of the industry and specific task you decide to check out. Maybe Frank has been holding on to a great idea, just waiting to share and it changes things for the better. Be open-minded in your discovery with employees.

Is there a need for change?

I suppose the emphasis around this, is this person right for the role? Is this the best and highest use for them? Have they been doing this for far too long that monotony has set in, their complacent or is it the right time to have a change? Is it time to change up the staff to do a bit of a rotation that invigorates the crew, and will that motivate them, or will it have a more demoralising effect?

Ultimately, if you have this machine at the end of the day, is Frank the right person to be operating it or is it Lisa or a completely new hire?

As you go through each employee and to recap part of the Corporate Engine Optimiser questioning earlier, who is the right person for the right role at the right time?

If the answer is, it's not them then don't procrastinate, or let business plateau and be mediocre, give it a supercharge and take the time and effort to fix it. Be serious about getting it right; otherwise, you will not save your business from yourself if it turns out you are the lazy one just going along for the ride.

WHAT VALUE IS CREATED?

Are your employees creating value for your company?

Does the value they create outweigh the costs of their employment?

These two questions are two of the most pivotal questions any employer can ask. Providing value is what a company ultimately gets paid for. If they stop providing value, people will cease to pay for their products or services.

The value a company provides begins with the Boss and right through to each employee level. In order for a company to be successful, each employee must create enough value to outweigh the cost of employing them. If each employee isn't contributing to revenue and providing value as assigned to the role they are to perform and outcome expected, then it will have a knock-on effect to the overall value (and available resources) the company has.

Yet the value created by one's staff is one of the most difficult things to determine. Traditionally, the historical thinking of management has assumed that if someone is at work, in their office, then they are a good and productive employee.

Yes, they should be busy working and highly productive too. But are they doing the right things? Are they producing results? Are they creating value? These questions are much harder to answer but much more significant to quantify, and that is why reporting, KPI's performance-based measurables for each employee, each department are essential regardless of the role they perform. People have to be measured along with every other metric of the business.

The idea that an employee that is being productive and creating value as long as they are working long and hard is nothing short of delusional, yet it is far too easy an assumption to make. There needs to be a breakdown of the cost per sale, for example, and what steps in reverse are taken for the deal to occur. The cost of the widget delivered, the materials to make the widget, the labour to produce it, the cost of the machinery, the time of the employees to manage the process and create the widget, the salesperson who sells the widget, the marketing team who produce the campaign, the cost of the campaign to generate leads, the number of calls to be made to qualify and convert leads to prospects to qualified appointments, the cost to running the business, the overheads, the building lease, electricity, stationery and just keep adding more and more, even toilet rolls for the bathroom. Holy heck, that's a lot, right? You should know all of this!

Everything has a cost to run the operation that when the core costs are reviewed, and a cost per sale is quantified, for example, then one can work through the KPIs required against a specific role to attribute some value to the function to that person to 'pay for their seat' so to speak. It is quite an eye-opening exercise, one that all too often you want to close your eyes, put it in the 'too hard basket' and say wake me up when it looks better.

For example, a real estate company that sells a house and land package to their client base had a business analyst go through the costs involved with almost a fine-tooth comb, factoring in many of the things mentioned above, including commissions to the salespeople, property agent and so forth and revealed it was a staggering $24,000 cost per sale.

When this was shared with the entire team from marketing to customer service to event managers to sales staff and so on, there was more than just an oh shit moment, but also an appreciation for just how valuable a client was and to pull out all stops to provide a premium service. Before this, it was just a number plucked out of thin air and was never considered important. It changed the dynamic considerably and enabled more closely monitored performance measures for team results from the conversion of a prospect to client and their journey with the company.

Furthermore, it was also analysed that a repeat sale was circa $13,000. Therefore, much emphasis was placed on a strong referral program, including a VIP rewards program to take great care of the clients and have them repeat purchase. The results were amazing on many levels, not to mention more profit per transaction.

Another example several years ago, was a friend of mine had an employee who worked 50+ hours per week. He was always busy when working, and he was loyal and committed. However, after two years, according to him, he finally figured out that there was a huge negative gap in the actual value created from his hard work. Simply put, his activities did not create the amount of revenue necessary to sustain his position. For over two years he had virtually been shelling out his income without any substantial return on the investment.

Over the years, he has observed people like his former employee; generally, hard workers with good intentions. They truly believe that what they do is important and that their activities are essential to the success of the company. Business owners and managers often reinforce these beliefs by not regularly evaluating whether or not their activities actually produce value and they cruise along thinking all is just sweet.

Value is not necessarily always created by activity. Certain activities positively impacting customers, generating revenue, controlling expenses, or helping compliance with regulatory authorities clearly create some measure of value.

Activities must create value worth paying for. As a manager or business owner, you must know how to determine the value, not just the quantity or even efficiency, of the activities of your employees.

And you must know how to help redirect your employees' attention to more valuable activities when you discover their time spent is merely looking busy, but not productive.

That is to ensure their highest and best use. There are no passengers allowed.

HOW TO MEASURE VALUE

Whether you are the Boss or a manager trying to determine the value of what your staff members do or an individual who wants to create more value with your activities, here is a list of things you can do to measure value. This Value Analysis process can help you separate activities that create value from those that just keep people busy.

1. For each position, or for yourself, write down the goals that are important to the position or to you right now. As a Boss, these goals should identify the key deliverables and results of your company or a specific department for which you involve any relevant management.

2. Track your activities and those of that department for one to two weeks. The level of detail can be relatively quickly noted. For example, the record for a full eight hour day might have 10-15 macro key points covering the entire workday.

3. At the end of the timeframe you set, create a chart summarizing the various activities and the time spent on them. The report should break down these activities into key categories that enable you to pinpoint the areas similar to those in the Corporate Engine Optimiser you ran through earlier or those applicable to your company operations and give a good snapshot.

4. Review the data. Are there activities you are doing that have no apparent value? Or is the amount of time spent on some activities far in excess of the value created? If

you are doing this for your department or your business, discuss the time spent on each activity with others in management. Is everything that is being produced creating the intended value?

5. Finally, as you look at the analysis, consider the following:

Are there activities that used to have value but now they no longer do?

Do some activities represent pet projects of leadership but have no real value to the company? If so, review the analysis with leadership and decide to keep going or stop it.

Is your perception of value consistent with the market and others you work with?

What are the results and value of those activities? Don't get caught up in the activities themselves. Results create value; activities are costs.

What areas is time being majorly spent on? What is the real value created? Can less time be spent to achieve similar results? Can a person (junior vs. senior in terms of salary) do some, or all, of the task? Is this an internal role, or should it be outsourced?

Remember that you can use the value analysis on an ongoing basis to evaluate your effectiveness and the productivity of your employees. Keep in mind that time is the most valuable resource you and your staff have.

Individuals who focus their time on key areas to create value, achieve far greater success than those who do not.

Therefore, it is essential that you know what creates value for your company, what does not, and where changes need to be made. Seems obvious right? It is, yet not often actioned. So actually, try it out.

AS PREVIOUSLY MENTIONED, IDENTIFY THE PERSONALITY OF PEOPLE YOU HAVE EMPLOYED AT YOUR WORKPLACE USING BEHAVIOURAL TESTING, PSYCHOMETRIC ANALYSING AND POTENTIAL MINING ALONG WITH PERFORMANCE REVIEWS REGULARLY.

Identify the Player Profiles within your organisation, right people, right role, right time - focused on professional and productive outcomes. No passengers allowed!

Your focus as Boss, as a Leader, is to run a successful business, turning great revenue, making a profit, and to supply a need to the consumer, delighting them so they come back for more while telling others they should do business with you too.

To provide that supply (widget/service, etc.) you highly likely require a workforce - a skilled one, trained (can be trained), professional, productive, show up to work, values their work and contributes to a great work culture, that you as Boss have created and damn well wish to maintain. Right?

As Boss, you need to provide a culture of productivity and excellence that pays good, even better for above performance, reward and recognise great employees, allow championing of ideas, support, and teamwork are paramount and highly encouraged.

Turnover of staff is instability for a company and the expense to recruit, onboard and train them is costly and time-consuming before finding out whether you have a keeper or a creeper, meaning someone who is just cruising along with no care or interest in the role.

It's just a job. And job stands for just over broke for many, a boring means to an end, not exciting or motivating, let alone interesting, and all too often if it is just a job to them, it can become miserable to show up to work, then they start pulling sickies here and there and becoming lackadaisical at work.

Everyone has their off days, no doubt about it, that's life. But it should not become a habit at work and that others must carry this person. Why put up with this shit?

It's not okay!

THEIR FULL POTENTIAL

A plan to maximise an employee's full potential. A personal development program designed to build confidence and maximize leadership and teamwork potential in employees. The plan is developed in alignment with the mission, values, and culture of an employee's organization in order to protect the investment made in the hiring process and for the role in which they are to perform.

The objective of realising their full potential is twofold:

1. Improve employee retention rates for the company by offering opportunities for employees to excel in their positions and to feel as if they are a vital contributor and offer reward and recognition.

2. Guide employees to live up to their full potential and to which they touted at the interview, that they would perform in their role and not be a passenger.

This program is intended to be administered by leaders who will maintain confidentiality for each employee along with encouragement and support.

The program consists of five phases:

- Assessment
- Reality Check
- The Plan
- Rehearsal
- Celebration

1. Assessment

The Leader must have a working knowledge of the company's mission, goals, culture, and organizational structure. They will meet with each employee who is participating in the program and conduct a thorough assessment of their professional goals as aligned within the context of the company.

2. Reality Check

The Leader will meet with other senior management to review the employee's personnel evaluation and to recommend any training needed. From those discussions and reports, the Leader, in collaboration with the employee can create an action plan.

3. The Plan

What follows next is customised training for the employee which may include the development of certain skills such as presentation skills, technical skill improvements, listening and asking the right questions, networking, negotiating, language strengthening, leadership skills, professionalism, career direction and the list goes on. The employee may be referred to highly skilled consultants to help them excel in their role. Throughout the Plan phase, the employee will be assigned specialised training.

4. Rehearsal

The employee will have specific assignments to accomplish and will practice, practice, practice. Forums will be suggested in which they may practice/demonstrate all they have learned. For instance, if an employee is asked to improve their presentation skills, they may be asked to research a relevant topic and make a special presentation to colleagues.

5. Celebration

Not all employees want special recognition, but every employee wants to feel appreciated. The Leader of the program must ask each employee how they are best motivated. That will give guidance on the best ways to keep employees motivated and developed. It does not mean you follow through with all their princess wishes, but some may be easily implementable, and nothing better than being in agreeance with what they said drives them and hold them accountable to that also.

Besides, it gives more buy-in from the employee.

There must be effective methods your company can use to celebrate the good work your employees have shown. The celebrations should reward their achievements.

POSITIVE TEAM CONFLICT

We know from personal and professional relationships that there is conflict, that is good and bad and it's about sorting through it all to extract that which is helpful, constructive and productive and not just bitter unhelpful, negative fighting.

While the word conflict immediately connotates negative, combat and more, it is the healthy conflict that can help the team.

People who are encouraged to speak up, debate various concepts, dissect an idea, product, or service and be critical about it, yet focusing on actually looking for a solution that is agreed to and all input has been heard, is constructive criticism and likely positive conflict.

Workplace conflict of a harmful kind is not to be tolerated in any way, shape or form. Ensure you have a substantial clause in the employment contract that deals with this and use it, in conjunction with your legal advisers to move the employee out the door.

However, conflict with a purpose for a good robust discussion to allow the team to share their ideas whether others agree or disagree is valuable to hear all sides.

Having everyone share their perspective can give management a good inside look into the makeup of the team and those who may very well be the producers of that product, or service or be at the selling end of it all.

Without their input, and a team resolution and buy-in from all, you end up having an employee who feels shunned, not listened to and affects their attitude to their work and the output, team spirit, culture and more begins to suffer in the workplace environment.

It's not about negative personal comments to one another, nor any aggressiveness to one another is tolerated, but it's expected there will be disagreement, passionate somewhat heated debate for sure, so long as it is in a good spirit and any dispute is talked through of each other's pro and cons and to form a consensus to move forward.

There will undoubtedly be those with the more direct behavioural style which may very well try and steer the conversation their way or to get support for their point of view, however with good leadership; one can encourage even the quietest, introverted employee, who may very well have the secret to solving it all, speak up, so let all voices be heard.

It is important to have a plan to handle anyone who wants to control the meeting. Have equal time set aside for each person to state their comments, acknowledge the contribution, and not immediately dismiss it, if it is not of your view.

Pull into line others who may jump on that person's comment in a retaliatory type of way and remind the team it is not to be personal but to allow everyone to share and we will consider each comment as it pertains to 'x' product or 'y' service or 'z' decision we are making and come to a formal team agreement. You will need a good referee in this meeting.

This positive conflict can help team meetings be more interesting (yes, we have all sat in on boring as you know what type meetings), enable the sharing of more ideas and encourages everyone to speak up and be heard. It helps to get an issue out in the open and everyone tackle it, work through to a general consensus and move on to the next.

It shows that leadership is interested in the contribution of all team members and involves them in potential areas they may have no direct involvement or typical say so, yet sometimes those out of left field ideas from so-called outsiders looking in can be game-changers.

Don't make it personal, no negative combat allowed. Let everyone speak up and be heard and see how your meetings end up and more importantly, the production that results from it.

BY THE BOOK

From the outset it was mentioned that you would need to ensure you have top-notch legal counsel, experts in employment law to ensure you do everything by the book and so you don't come unstuck in the process.

Different countries, states, laws, different workplace rules etc. very much prescribe legally what you can or cannot do. Even the most unproductive, laziest, try and touch me employee has rights.

There is a whole gamut of things that need to be navigated to ensure an exit of a lazy f@#k employee is carried out swiftly, with professionalism with all i's dotted and t's crossed, and a few prayers said so there is no further detriment to the business post an employee exit. Hell has no fury like an employee scorned.

Yes, tread carefully in this space, but when you know you have it all sorted, and they have no leg to stand on, then you invoke 'Devil mode' and deal with it fast. It's called that for a reason because somewhere during that exit meeting, they may very well tell you to go to hell anyway besides lots of other choice words.

It is why so many businesses just go with the flow and try and ignore it and brush it off rather than face confrontation. Yet they wonder why good employees don't stick around for long. Well, get a grip mate, because they see firsthand how these lazy f@#k or worse, employees run the show.

This is the unpleasant side of running a business, but it's time to take out the trash.

GET IT TOGETHER BOSS

- You need to trust your people and give them the benefit of the doubt that they are good workers and treat them fair and well, so it is reciprocal unless proven otherwise.
- Treat your client lists and other sensitive data like it's your only child. Put definite plans in place so a pissed off employee can't screw with it, and an idiot employee can't accidentally leak it.
- Put some clear policies around employee standards of behaviour and their job expectations. You must be very clear about what you expect from your employees. Ensure this is in the employment contract and reiterated at performance reviews and so forth.
- Often overlooked but equally as important is to have a straightforward process around what happens when employees stuff up and what happens when mistakes are made versus negligence or worse.

YOU GOTTA DO THIS

- As Leaders, one of the most challenging issues we deal with is the engagement and productivity of our employees. If you fear an employee exodus when the economy heats up and people are jumping to what they perceive as greener grass (better deal, pay, etc.) then you owe it to yourself and your company to become a sought after employer where people want to work and be a part of.
- You identify your target markets, your target customers, and your target growth areas. Why not identify your target employee? Identify the combination of thinking style and behavioural traits that build success and engagement in your company that attract and keep them.
- Hire and promote to those traits and you will create an engaged workforce that will sing your praises and put you on your way to a preferred 'I want to work there' employer status.

THIS PAGE IS LEFT INTENTIONALLY BLANK

Why?

Because you've just assessed if your workplace culture and the environment is good or garbage, now it's time to check what you have on your team and if it is a shitshow or not.

PLAYER PROFILES
THE TEAM MIX UP

THE DOZEN PLAYER PROFILES

In order to try and correct your dysfunctional team, you first need to work out what the f@#k is going on - and who the f@#k do you have working in your business?

My scientific system (working for and consulting with a f@#king lot of businesses and observing a considerable amount of people in various work environments, not to mention a large amount of research and input from all sorts of people) has boiled down to these 12 'players' you need to be aware of - and to sort out.

It's time to identify the problem 'players' you have in your business. And GO, GET, FU!

THE FIRST HALF DOZEN PLAYER PROFILES	PLAYER NUMBER

THE ANGEL

01

THE LAZY F@#K

02

THE MOODY F@#K

03

THE SOOKY BUBBA

04

THE CONTROL FREAK

05

THE BULLY

06

THE SECOND HALF DOZEN PLAYER PROFILES	PLAYER NUMBER
 THE SCHEMER	**07**
 THE BULLSHIT ARTIST	**08**
 THE BOSSY BRITCHES	**09**
 THE SICKIE	**10**
 THE YOU CAN'T TOUCH THIS	**11**
 THE DEVIL	**12**

THE ANGEL

BLESS THEIR LITTLE HEART

(FU) **angel**
Your Workplace, Anywhere

⋮

01

01

118,378 views
angel so lovely at the office today #angel
View all 1,237 comments
1 JANUARY

PLAYER 01 - THE ANGEL

Who's your Angel? Most likely, the first person that popped into your mind when you read that line. The Angel is the person you like the most in your organisation because they like you. They're dependable, punctual, and generally meet deadlines. They also make you feel good about yourself; every idea you have is a great idea. Every decision you make is brilliant! (Spoiler alert. It's not!)

They are an absolute Angel. There's nothing they won't do for you. They are the best at kissing ass, and you're okay with it. They could very well be a wolf under that innocent sheep's clothing, and you don't see it, it doesn't even register on your radar, sadly. They are playing a great stealth game. They know an enormous amount about you and the business. If you are one of those loose gooses that dump all your personal shit on social media, then they are trolling you. Of course, they are gathering intel and storing it for a rainy day. Well not exactly - more so when it's time to apply leverage to get what they want - pay rise being an obvious agenda. Not all Angels are undercover, and some do have a halo, just have to sort out who.

The Angel employee is by far the easiest to manage. They pretty much follow every instruction because they want to impress. It doesn't mean the Angel is either good or bad at their work, just that if they are bad, the fact they are so obedient to the process, cheerful and more, let's your guard down and they seem always to get cut some slack.

They are so tuned in you could just hand them the keys and go on an extended holiday, because they are so nice, accommodating, even reasonably productive. Much of it is superficial, after all, that 'less work more pay' can be quite true.

It goes both ways though, and if an Angel employee gets treated so much better than the others, the two issues are on the boil; 1. When it comes time to put your foot down and apply more workload, etc., it will be seen as "why me", "what have I done wrong?" 2. others in the team will easily see this and that you have chosen your favourites. It is important to keep an eye on the Angel behaviour.

What does an Angel employee look like? Check these out:

- ✓ Brings in food for the team - with a special one just for you.
- ✓ Is never late with their weekly reports.
- ✓ Friends you on social media (and likes everything you post).
- ✓ Organises the birthday cards for the whole office.
- ✓ Happy to work late - especially if it's to help a team member or more importantly you.
- ✓ Really wants to be liked - especially by you!
- ✓ Dresses nicely - but not in the most on-trend fashions.
- ✓ Likes to volunteer for charities in their spare time (and they're not afraid to tell you about it!).
- ✓ Knows that Simon in accounts has an allergy to pistachios.
- ✓ Has been known to offer free massages (um okay).
- ✓ Looks after drunk Harry at the Christmas Party.
- ✓ Probably didn't get enough love as a child.
- ✓ Annoys the f@#k out of you (without any apparent reason for it).

At their best, Angel employees are reliable, steadfast members of your team. They'll never be your superstars as they're too busy trying to make everyone like them. If you can deal with the constant ingratiating, and other employees don't scare them away, you have a good employee who will work hard to keep your ship sailing okay and won't cause a mutiny.

But beware. What's the opposite of an Angel? The Devil, that's what! Your lovely, suck up Angel has the potential to become the spawn of Satan. When you get to 'Player 12', you will learn more about your Angel who's turned Devil, and how they're affecting your business.

The Angel Boss

Yes indeed. Some bosses are Angels too! The Angel Boss is a dream for employees - particularly the Lazy F@#Ks and Sooky Bubbas. The Angel Boss is a f@#king nightmare for your business, though. If you're an Angel Boss, let me remind you - the boss can't be everyone's friend, you needy idiot!

An Angel Boss is a godsend. Some may call them a pushover, asleep at the wheel, or you can think of a few terms yourself to describe this. An Angel Boss is a dream for lazy f@#k employees because there are very few times they will be appropriately managed, let alone monitor their performance, production, and professionalism. It's party time, almost daily.

If you relate to any or all of these points, you're The Angel Boss (and congratulations, it's all your fault):

✓ You know, intimately, the private lives and issues of every employee.

✓ Use the phrase "that's OK" at least 20 times a day.

✓ You volunteer for charities in your spare time (and tell your staff all about it via the company newsletter).

✓ Have a Management team of underperformers (because you've never fired anyone in your life, and you reward loyalty).

✓ You have a funny feeling your staff are taking the piss, but you ignore it.

✓ You could dress well, but you don't, as you do not want to intimidate your staff.

✓ Your staff ARE taking the piss, and you're too scared to do anything about it.

✓ You've taken up boxing to help manage the frustration you feel at being taken advantage of (but you're having trouble hitting that bag).

✓ You're weak. AF.

You are the Angel that everyone loves, and you love them, every request they make or 'sorry I'm late' you go that's okay. You are the softie, giving in, oblivious to those shrewd ones taking full advantage of your generosity.

You may even socialise with them, more often paying for everything, almost because you think you need them as friends, so they like you. All the while, you are just being played subtly, and this becomes very hard to switch from friend to boss at any time when you need to.

Aaah what a nice Boss, is okay if we come in late, go early, even work from home today. Ah, thanks you're sooo lovely, you're also a softie, too nice of a person.

You are essentially almost in the friend zone or, so you think you are, but not quite. This is where you are being robbed blind, and don't realise it or cannot front up and acknowledge these ones are outsmarting you. Think about who pays their wage, pinch yourself, seriously pinch yourself. Feel some pain? Good, it represents the pain or that time and money drain that many of them are playing you for. Wake the f@#k up!

As for you, if you're the Angel Boss, you need to harden the f@#k up. Keep reading (as punishment) for ways to do it. And drink some cement in the meantime.

The Umpire's Rule - 95% Stay | 5% Gone

The Angel has redeemable qualities. They are one that can be moulded into a good contributing employee that you can work with now you have identified who they are and how they operate. Only if you see behavioural traits from the other more aggressive players sink in, then will you need to pull the Angel into line, performance manage them, which they will be most likely receptive to, in fact liking the attention somewhat if you deliver the message properly.

If they venture too far to the dark side, then you make that determination well before then, as you will be tuned into their behavioural traits and little tricks now, so no one pulls the wool over your eyes, right?

THIS PAGE IS LEFT INTENTIONALLY BLANK

Why?

So, you can list the Angels on the team,
say ahh, oh shit, okay I get it and toughen up for this next
one we reveal!

THE LAZY F@#K

GET OFF YOUR ASS

FU **lazyf@#k**
Your Workplace, Anywhere

02

02

86,678 views
lazyf@#k is it home time yet? #lazyf@#k
View all 2,721 comments
2 FEBRUARY

PLAYER 02 - THE LAZY F@#K

Repeat after me… "Oh Shit". The Lazy F@#K employees are everywhere, almost like a zombie apocalypse. If you have them on staff (and most do), this shit is not good. The Lazy F@#K employee does not go out of their way to show initiative, be a team player or fit well with the rest of the team unless you have hit rock bottom and they are all lazy f@#ks.

The other team members will have checked out this lazy f@#k a long time ago and be watching them as much as watching the Boss and whether they step up to do anything about it.

Your average Lazy F@#K employee is easy to spot. They actively avoid work wherever possible, and they're not subtle about it. They won't do anything that's 'not their job' and resist any tasks other than what they believe they were hired to do. They arrive precisely on time, take 20 minutes to start their computer, eat breakfast and chat.

It's not hard to spot your average Lazy F@#K, and if you have one, and you know it, and haven't done anything about them, then YOU need help, and you better study this guide and then some. Then f@#k off, sort them out and talk to me when you've fired that Lazy F@#Ker.

The Lazy F@#K sneaky employee, on the other hand, doesn't put much energy into anything, except making you think they're the hardest working motherf@#ker in your company.

They are crafty little f@#kers, never missing an opportunity to tell you how 'overworked' they are or take all the credit for somebody else's work. They're so crafty it can be challenging to identify one. Here are a couple of tips:

- ✓ First, look at all the people who you know that are really busy - especially the ones who are always telling you they're really busy.
- ✓ Ask lots of questions about work they're claiming they did, and their job in general. The Lazy F@#K is very good at claiming other team members work - but they're so lazy they often don't know WTF it's all about.

Other characteristics of your Lazy F@#K employee are:

- ✓ They are always plagued with computer issues - usually right around deadlines.
- ✓ A lot of your other staff truly despise them - especially people below them in the hierarchy usually, because they've been ripping off their work, praise, bonus, and promotions!
- ✓ The most used phrase in their vocabulary is "I'm soooo busy at the moment". Usually finished with a big sigh, designed for maximum sympathy.
- ✓ In the past, they may have won your 'Employee of the Year' Award. They should be in politics - their PR bullshit is on point!
- ✓ They are the first to leave when you're not in the office.
- ✓ They will make a massive deal if they stay late - and if you were to check their browsing history, there would be a lot of social media trolling and online shopping getting done!

✓ It's difficult for you to describe what exactly they do. It's lots of huffing and puffing and use of a few key phrases like 'reporting period', 'server capacity' and '_____'. By the way, that's their plan. You can't pinpoint a f@#king enigma.

A Lazy F@#K of any kind is never at their best. There is not a lot of good about a Lazy F@#K employee. They may have some redeeming features, but do you want to spend time finding out? They've spent years honing their craft of being a lazy f@#k. Make them walk the plank. NOW! (And make sure that lazy f@#k doesn't get someone else to do it for them).

The Lazy F@#K as Boss

Really? If you're one of these sad creatures; 1. How the f@#k did you get to become a business owner in the first place? And 2. Sell up and F off. You're an imposter. And a real idiot. Your sneaky lazy f@#kery is mainly hurting you. What the actual f@#k!

A Lazy F@#K Boss is an Angel Boss that just doesn't give a toss. Whether the business is going under, or they have serious personal issues that have just overwhelmed them or daydreaming about escaping the role, the Lazy F@#K Boss needs to have a quiet word from someone else in the organisation that carries any authority or sensibility that can talk directly to the Lazy F@#K Boss and get them to sort their shit out pronto. The entire team is waiting to see their next move, so harden the f@#k up and lead the team and run the business already.

Anything is worth trying to turn this person around; otherwise, it's a doom and gloom ending and lets everyone run wild at work.

The Umpire's Rule - 41% Stay | 59% Gone

The Lazy F@#K is almost a coin toss in that a performance review, some training and additional attention can possibly turn them around. If you have determined that they have some good qualities that do add to the team, then run them through the Get Fired Up Flow in the next section. If there is no evidence of a change of behaviour, then they will just sink further into lazy land, and you exit them for not meeting targets.

Ensure everything is well documented in the performance review, backed up by your solid employment contract; otherwise, you will begin to spawn an aggressor you do not need and sure as shit do not want on the team.

THIS PAGE IS LEFT INTENTIONALLY BLANK

Why?

Ahh, we just got started, so make some notes on how you will deal with these ones.
Take a deep breath; it gets worse.

THE MOODY F@#K

CHEER UP WILL YA

moodyf@#k
Your Workplace, Anywhere

03

MOODY
F@#K

03

170,118 views
moodyf@#k I am not in a mood today #moodyf@#k
View all 8,187 comments
3 MARCH

PLAYER 03 - THE MOODY F@#K

Yikes! The Moody F@#K employee is hard to deal with, mainly because you never know what to expect from them. If, for instance, they were an asshole consistently at least you'd know what to expect and have the ability to prepare accordingly. The Moody F@#K is maddeningly inconsistent - an absolute Angel at 9.45 am, and a cold-hearted Bully by 10 am! Generally, though, they'll always be consistently professional and even-tempered with you. That's how you know they can control their f@#king moods; they're just choosing not to most of the time.

The Moody F@#K employee is a major downer on the positive work environment. You could say pretty much anything, including "Good morning", and it is received with a next to nothing positive reply, more like a hmm yeah whatever, as they are just so disinterested and disengaged. The Moody F@#K employee has a lot of shit going on in their personal life, of which may never be known in the workplace, but they sure as shit bring it to work and mope around the office, counter any positive talk with negative, and are dragging down the rest of the team. If you want to build a corporate culture of positive teamwork, get the job done, and have a reward, then the Moody F@#K employee is not one to have on the team.

Moody F@#K employees are a conundrum. As far as their production goes, they're just OK. Being semi-efficient at their actual tasks is partly what has allowed them to get away with being such a f@#king asshole to deal with (save the few hours a week they're being a delight). They have a severe effect on your company culture and office morale, though! Most importantly, they're preventing an open communication flow.

Work out who your Moody F@#Ks are by watching how your other employees interact with them. Check this out:

✓ Junior employees especially will often cringe around them, for no apparent reason.
✓ Most people will avoid challenging them in meetings (or otherwise).
✓ Some mornings they won't say hello to anyone, other mornings they can't wait to hear how everyone's evening was! They will receive short non-committal answers.
✓ They won't talk to many people at the Christmas Party - or rather not many people will speak to them!

Other indicators that you have a Moody F@#K employee in your midst include:

✓ General unease when they walk in a room.
✓ The Moody F@#K employee might feel their disdain of most people is justified because they do all the work and everyone else is a f@#kwit.

The Moody F@#K as Boss

The Moody F@#K Boss is a train wreck. Two-fifths of f all work is getting done because they are preoccupied with other more pressing, more personal stuff that is consuming their lives. The missus is screwing the neighbour, a big tax debt, company in financial trouble, drug addiction, gambling problems, could be a whole myriad of things.

If you're a Moody F@#K Boss, you'll most likely never admit it to yourself (or, only if your mood takes a self-introspection bent. And we all know that will only last until lunchtime when you remember how much you hate it when people say hello, and then dramatically slam your office door to make sure everyone in the office knows that.

If you're feeling even slightly introspective, check to see if any of these apply to you:

You tend to hear about problems last, and only if you must hear about them.

There are usually 1 or 2 people who interact with you the most, and they often speak on behalf of other staff.

You have a sneaking suspicion you never get the full story.

There will be tears in the office at least once a week - and it's not just a coincidence that interaction with you is the common denominator.

For your Secret Santa, you received actual prescription medication for bipolar patients. There were audible gasps when you opened it, and the organiser of the gift was unexpectedly absent for the rest of the week!

Speaking earlier of open communication flows. If you're a Moody F@#K Boss, forget about it. Your fickle moods have made you unapproachable. Your staff will do almost anything to avoid talking with you. Especially if they need to let you know, there is a problem, or there is a massive f@#k up that you need to know about! It's your fault. You better fix that shit.

Where you start to realise enough is enough and push back a little, this is usually met with some slight resistance though cleverly disguised bewilderment. You hear the water cooler chat 'she's a real bitch today...must be that time of the month aye' and you'd be well justified to walk up to them and say FU.

This is where those days of superwoman/superman kick in, and you state that you're not going to put up with any bullshit today. You bark orders, ruffle those mighty sales staff peacock feathers, or burst that sensitive princess admin team bubble. You're now quickly evaluated as to your levels of mean.

I know I know - you aren't quite ready to turn up the heat. Hang on, though, let's keep moving along and dial it up further before you throw in the towel and give up.

Otherwise, you might as well announce that the team can run the business while you wake up to the fact that they are already running the business - right into the proverbial f'in ground.

The Umpire's Rule - 34% Stay | 66% Gone

The Moody F@#K is an interesting one. There is so much going on in life, many challenges and a lot of that is not known by you or others in the workplace, yet their moody attitude sure is. Perhaps you can glean from others on the team in a caring, interested not outright nosey way to see if it is work-related or personal.

Tread carefully, though. Otherwise, depending on their demeanour, you can have a meeting to see how they are and show empathy and be genuine.

Be careful as this can be a powder keg ready to go off if you have misread it. It could be something that is fixable, and if so, it turns them around. Your input could be their saving grace and builds another level of the nice boss now helping them be a nicer employee.

If the Moody F@#K just carries a permanent same shit different day mood attitude, then it's time to review their performance, etc. and manage that appropriately, likely out the door. Similarly, with others, they can quickly change, so watch closely, but do not be caught spying on them; otherwise, you will escalate to a level you absolutely do not want.

THIS PAGE IS LEFT INTENTIONALLY BLANK

Why?

Because now you are starting to get agitated that there are
some players on your team,
and we are only warming up.

THE SOOKY BUBBA

THAT'S ENOUGH ALREADY

sookybubba
Your Workplace, Anywhere

04

04

26,984 views

sookybubba the world is picking on me #sookybubba

View all 2,937 comments

4 APRIL

PLAYER 04 - THE SOOKY BUBBA

The Sooky Bubba employee can pretty much be anyone at any time as we have all gone through shit that gets to us, and as human beings, the waterworks sprinkler turns on, it's natural. But it is more than that with the Sooky Bubba employee being so affected by things in their life, that can trigger them to breakdown and cry, and it's not just an isolated event, say the death of their beloved pet, or that their girlfriend or boyfriend dumped them, but almost every little thing can set them off. Others walk on tiptoes around them, careful not to be blamed for saying or doing something that winds them up like a clock only to see them unwind all emotional and at times inconsolably a wreck.

Everyone knows one or more of these. I'm talking about those that bring all their personal shit to work, mope around or play sooky bubba or have at work tanty moments. You know the ones; "I think my man is screwing someone else", "My wife has taken up bike riding, but I think she's riding the neighbour", "I'm going through a mid-life crisis", "My kids are playing up", "I'm not into it today". Yes, you heard it right, personal shit has sucked any sense of quality out the window. It's showing up to work to reach out to one's colleagues, build the sooky army and to hell with being productive today. Now hang on before you say hey wank, we all have our moments, and I couldn't agree more. That's why we have personal days, holidays, or even sick days provided, so have them take one and stay the f@#k away from spewing non-work-related garbage at work.

You already know who the Sooky Bubba employee in your midst is. The person who immediately sucks all the air, energy, and happiness from the room when they enter. At first, you thought they were just having a bad day. But a bad day has since stretched out to a bad year for them - and if YOU are a real f@#king moron, it's since stretched into a bad f@#king decade for your business. That's years and years of drama and misery that you and your staff are dealing with, and your business, ultimately, is paying the price. Nice job, dickhead!

As I said, you know who the Sooky Bubba is, but let's make some bullet points about them, just for fun - god knows you need it since they've been sucking the fun out of everything for years!

If you have a Sooky Bubba employee:

✓ They will always know where the tissues are.
✓ You should take a look at the office spend on tissues. It will be high!
✓ You should take notes and turn their daily dramas into a soap opera.
✓ On second thought, don't bother. It's boring, predictable shit. Plus, you will pay for it.
✓ For fun, try unloading some personal shit on them. It will freak them out. No again.
✓ F@#k no. A Sooky Bubba employee is not fun. Take this shit seriously. They're sucking the life out of you.

The Sooky Bubba as Boss

The Sooky Bubba Boss is a sad state of affairs and does not help show strong leadership to the team. You too have your moments, and yes, we're all human, and shit happens, however so long as you keep that away from the prying eyes and tuned in ears of your staff then you can have your sooky bubba moment in private, then shake it off, game face on and push forward.

Notwithstanding that stuff happens to everyone and that everyone processes and deals with it differently when it comes to working, and they are always upset is a real problem. Others need to step up and show leadership while having a heart-to-heart conversation with the Sooky Bubba Boss. It may just be a difficult moment or a passing phase, or if it is constant then some help, professional help is needed. Pronto!

If this is you, and you're the boss, what's up? Are you running a crèche or a f@#king business? Your employees aren't paid to listen to your shit; they are paid to work and to help make your business successful. You know, so you're not such a sooky bubba!

Seriously though. If you're in charge and constantly share your dramas with your employees, not only are you spreading misery, and being unproductive, you're putting yourself in a seriously compromised position. Some wily, sneaky, manipulative Devil employee is no doubt ferreting away all this personal information that you're leaking, to use in some dastardly way in the future.

Here's the thing. People Talk Gossip, especially in a work environment. Even if you've just shared your sooky worries and dramas with one (apparently) trusted confidante in the office, it's most likely that everyone

112

knows what's going on with you - even the guy who delivers the water.

At best, your employees will not view you as the motivating, inspirational leader they want to believe in. At worst, think about what that sneaky, underhanded, Devil employee can do with the following information:

- ✓ You are concerned that you're not as smart as people think.
- ✓ Last year, you attended counselling for drug addiction.
- ✓ You're upset that you might have to rethink the HR team because they're just not on your side.
- ✓ You've considered selling the business because it is causing problems at home.
- ✓ You suspect your wife/husband/partner is cheating on you with your best friend (you're 'devastated' but hopeful it will end soon).

You need to shut your mouth and stop leaking your personal information before you f@#k things up any further.

The Umpire's Rule - 31% Stay | 69% Gone

If you're thinking you might be able to 'fix' your Sooky Bubba employee, think again. That's what got you here in the first place. There is a place for a pinch of compassion in the workplace, but it's unlikely there's enough compassion in the world to 'fix' your Sooky Bubba employee. Even if they perform well in their job, they're not performing to their full potential - by the simple fact that they're spending a considerable amount of time sharing their issues with their colleagues or sitting quietly at their desk focusing on their dramas, not their job.

The Sooky Bubba can be the next manifestation of the Moody F@#K and needs to be looked at, to understand why they act this way. Your role is not one of a Shrink, but to genuinely be interested in your team as one affects many. Similarly, to the Moody F@#K, follow similar reconnaissance to ascertain if potentially fixable or got to go.

THIS PAGE IS LEFT INTENTIONALLY BLANK

Why?

The nicer of the bunch, if we can call them that are out of the way, now we venture into not so good space. Hold on!

THE CONTROL FREAK

CALM THE F@#K DOWN

controlfreak
Your Workplace, Anywhere

⋮

05

CONTROL
FREAK

05

170,915 views

controlfreak just do what I tell you to do #controlfreak

View all 5,861 comments

5 MAY

PLAYER 05 - THE CONTROL FREAK

Ahhh - the Control Freak employee. What an incredible, useful, and altogether insecure as f@#k employee your average Control Freak is!

The Control Freak employee is an absolute pain in the ass. Bordering on Bully, even a sprinkle of Devil and this person is much worse than Bossy Britches. They want to control everything; the project is theirs, and they make it known they are running the show. Even stupid shit like it is their parking space, their coffee cup, the specific items they claim are for them and not to mention they try and butt in and take over conversations.

The guiding principle of the Control Freak employee is to make themselves irreplaceable. Inevitably, this manifests in them being ridiculously sensitive about sharing any part of their job role, as well as being stupidly secretive.

Another, more sinister reason is that the Control Freak employee might need to be closely watched what they actually do in YOUR business, so keep a close eye on your data, client list and intellectual property. Let's just say it's to do with being a Lazy F@#K. Go straight to the Lazy F@#K section if you think your employee's control freakiness ISN'T coming from a place of insecurity. Here's more about the insecure Control Freak.

A Control Freak employee:

✓ Hates going on holidays! They're terrified someone will take over their job.

✓ F@#ks your business over with their insecurity. They will never hand over any information about the tasks they do. Consequently, any leave - particularly unplanned leave - will result in customers being left hanging, and in the worst case, your office not being able to function because nobody (but old Control Freak) knows how to get hold of the person that sorts out your internet issues.

✓ Is f@#king annoying.

✓ Would prefer to answer emails from the hospital than share a single shred of knowledge.

✓ Is f@#king annoying.

✓ Sighs a lot. Mainly because they end up having to do lots of easy tasks for the office - stuff anyone with a tiny bit of information could do.

✓ Is a really f@#king annoying idiot.

The Control Freak as Boss

If you're a Control Freak Boss, on the other hand, you're not guided by insecurity it's the opposite. The Control Freak Boss is all about Superiority. Their own. This is quite a common disorder amongst the founders of businesses. Not only is it your idea, time, money, sweat, tears and know-how that got the company where it is today - nobody could care about it as much as you. Your ego is through the roof, and you need to get it in check real damn fast pal.

The Control Freak Boss is pretty much a given if barking orders in the military, but in civilian workplaces is an absolute asshole. While it is understandable that the boss may just be protecting their 'baby', their oversight and control of the business, which at one level is fair enough to accept, it is the micro-managing, teeny weeny dot the i's and cross the t's, sticking their nose into everything that makes it so damn annoying. It is that lack of trust in others in management or supervision to handle all the operational minutia.

All bosses need a certain amount of the Control Freak in them, but with moderation. It's your vision, and you have the right to set the course. But remember. If your business is big enough to require more than a handful of employees, you physically can't control everything. You're not an idiot, so hopefully, you've made some good hiring decisions, and have at least some people in the right places. You hired them for their expertise. Let them f@#king do their thing.

Here are some signs you're taking Control Freakiness too far:

✓ High staff turnover. Talented people won't put up with being micromanaged.
✓ Your employees (the ones that do hang around) might often use the phrase 'please elaborate/clarify/confirm'. Translation: 'Be Clear. And Tell Me What the F@#k You Actually Want.'
✓ Despite being fully briefed and updated on projects, you'll often make a last-minute change that puts the timeline into absolute chaos.
✓ You have a sneaky feeling that you no longer inspire your employees, but you probably brush it off, thinking they're all f@#king morons, right?

Look, it can be a little bit advantageous for you to have a Control Freak employee amongst your ranks. They're willing to go to ridiculous lengths to keep their job 'safe'. But single point sensitivity isn't a joke. You can't afford for any employee to be indispensable. You need to sort that shit out and have a backup plan if it all goes south.

The Umpire's Rule - 22% Stay | 78% Gone

The Control Freak has some comparable traits to that of the Bossy Britches, in that their role as a manager, supervisor or team leader, for example, may just fuse with their ego and their directive to the team is so off-putting because it's like they have a workplace 'road rage' rev up that is uncalled for.

They need to have their own performance review incorporating some leadership training to tone them down and approach their delivery in a more team-driven, less militaristic order barking way. If there is no improvement, then they have all but opened the goodbye, see you later door for a mass employee exodus.

If they are not in a leadership or supervisory role, understand why they are so controlling and manipulative and pissing people off. If you get to the bottom of it and can train them to correct their behaviour, then good for you as that is pushing shit uphill to be frank. Otherwise, yes, it is what it is and bye-bye.

THIS PAGE IS LEFT INTENTIONALLY BLANK

Why?

Yes, you get the picture now what you have been putting up with, but wait, there's more. If you have these one's, well...

THE BULLY

TIMES UP ASSHOLE

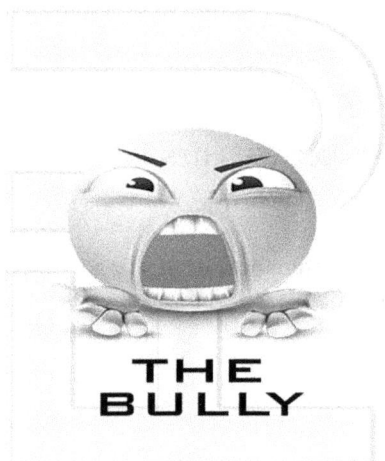

bully
Your Workplace, Anywhere

06

06

320,313 views
bully hurry up and do my work stuff too #bully
View all 9,801 comments
6 JUNE

PLAYER 06 - THE BULLY

You need to know who the Bully employee in your business is. And yes, that's purposely written in the singular. Unless you're a massive organisation with hundreds of employees, there is only room for one Bully in your business.

The Bully employee is just that, a bully who needs a good kick up the ass, taken out back and given some of their own medicine (quite ironic isn't it?) But seriously, we won't stoop to their level; instead, the Bully employee needs their marching orders without delay. Nothing is redeeming about them, time to go!

The Bully employee brings aggressive, standover, controlling behaviour and rips the head off any good workplace vibe. The Bully employee gets pleasure from picking on others, telling them what to do, poking fun at them, interfering in their work and much more. Most of it will be gossip because they are clever assholes at ensuring many don't witness their deplorable behaviour. Simply, the Bully employee must go. This piece of shit leopard does not change its spots.

For people on the same level or subordinate to them, the Bully employee will be overtly hostile. They can't help it. Making others feel like shit makes them horny. Seriously, they get off on it.

There's a school of thought that says you should empathise, get to know, and ultimately love your bully. Who hurt them when they were just a wee, innocent child? Are they caring for an abusive, sick grandparent that nobody knows about? Who. F@#king. Cares! In an ideal, politically correct, love everyone world that would be wonderful. Unicorns live in an ideal world, and I've NEVER seen a unicorn. Nor have you. You don't have time to love the Bully in your business, because they're hating it into the ground.

Unlike your Moody F@#K employee, your Bully employee doesn't even have a 'let's be kind to everyone' day (or even a minute). They're so f@#king mean to the core.

Here's how you can tell you have a Bully employee in your midst:

✓ High Tension, Tears & Turnover.
✓ There is an audible sigh of relief when they leave the room.
✓ When they're not in the office, it's down-right celebratory up in there!
✓ You've never actually seen them behave in a bullying way. (Bullies are sneaky, and genius at hiding their true nature).
✓ There's something about them that makes you feel uneasy (yes YOU, King of your little Empire).
✓ If they have a significant other, they rarely say a word at the office Christmas party (if they come at all).
✓ You'd be better off without them (you don't know that yet but take my word for it).

The Bully as Boss

Woah. You're everyone's worst nightmare. As the boss, you feel entitled to behave in ways that you would probably never get away with outside this little fiefdom you've created for yourself. You're probably a reasonably OK person outside of work, but the power at work has gone to your head. You love nothing more than seeing the peasants scurry and cower as you make your daily rounds, surveying your empire.

The Bully Boss is, to put it bluntly - an asshole. In nearly every situation if the boss is a bully, it breeds others in the organisation to be one too without fear of retribution or reprisal. In fact, thinking it is the norm and condoned.

Unless the Bully Boss seeks counselling and changes their ways, it is the employee that has to step away and right now. This is cause for a volatile workplace if not already, with no leadership, no respect, no team spirit, instead it's a negative shit environment that is doing no one any favours. It is a mindf@#k organisation, and the Bully Boss is to blame.

This bullish Bully behaviour extends beyond your staff. You treat outside contractors like crap regularly. Business partners are starting to drop off. They don't need your f@#king shit. Asshole. They're likely the only ones who will stand up to you. Your employees either shrink or cower to your bullshit. Or leave. Beware though. Your time will come.

By the way - if you have a Bully employee, and you're wondering why someone who is overtly displaying this really f@#ked up behaviour is still around, the reason is, you're allowing it! They're likely bullying you too. You just can't quite see it (they're much subtler with people higher in the pecking order). I won't haul you over the coals for this one - but now you know who the f@#king bully is you best put on your big pants and deal with them (Armour up, this will be war!)

The Umpire's Rule - 3% Stay | 97% Gone

In almost all cases, the Bully is history. Your employment contract and legal support should see to that. The tiny percentage of whether this is redeemable is whether they were the ones being bullied by someone else on the team and caught in the crossfire of them rightly given some oomph back. Not talking physically but standing up for themselves.

You will need to thoroughly ensure you have your facts about this one to see if that is the case. Then that is a meeting to discuss zero tolerance for that behaviour within the workplace. In all other instances, the Bully is history. That means clear them out today!

THIS PAGE IS LEFT INTENTIONALLY BLANK

Why?

Let me be the first to say sorry to you. Sorry, you just had that nightmare, NOT visionary daydream and realised HELP!

THE SCHEMER

YOUR GAME IS OVER

FU **schemer**
Your Workplace, Anywhere

⋮

07

THE
SCHEMER

07

◎ ◯ ◁ • • • ⊓

101,287 views
schemer ssh I have this great plan #schemer
View all 6,414 comments
7 JULY

PLAYER 07 - THE SCHEMER

Hold onto your hats jobs, people, the Schemer employee is here, and they want - well they want everything. A better office. Your 2IC's job. YOUR job! Worse, they want a piece of your other employees.

The Schemer employee is like the slick salesman, the poker shark, the jack of all trades, has the gift of the gab, knows all the contacts, been there, done that. They are the best at covering their ass and watching others get caught up in the crap that the Schemer has laid out for them as a smoke and mirror tactic to advance their own agenda.

These folks are everywhere, and they love the cat and mouse game. They think they are the cat, which leaves you, as the...? - you got it.

I'm not sure if I can do that. I'm not 100%. I haven't been trained to do that. Why can't Sam do that? I'm busy. It's not within my role and responsibilities. Blah blah.

Usually, a Middle to Senior Manager in your business, if that scheming f@#k put even half the effort into their job (the thing you pay them to do) as they do into their schemes, they probably could have your job. These guys are smart motherf@#kers, but they have pretty much gone to the dark side and chosen to use their not inconsiderable powers for evil instead of the good of your business.

What's worse? You have no idea. It's quite likely that they're your 'friend' outside of work. It's all part of their scheme - which is to GET EVERYTHING, remember?

As with the Lazy F@#K employee, it can be quite tricky to identify the Schemer employee. Unlike the Lazy F@#K, who just wants to coast along doing nothing much, on your dime, the Schemer has an agenda and a whole arsenal of tactics available, including:

- ✓ Outright claiming the work and ideas of other employees. How do they get away with it? - They share them with the important people (you) first. So, the employee who did the work has the choice of saying nothing or saying something (and risk looking small and petty). Most choose the former.
- ✓ Sneakily, if they're at war with another Manager (translation: if they want to steal the power, responsibilities, and salary of another Manager), they won't attack head-on. Instead, they will have one of their subordinates make a 'complaint' about one of the other Manager's team. They will then cause a fuss about it, making the other manager defend their staff member.
- ✓ By the way, you want Managers who defend and speak highly of their team. It's a sign that they're a human, not a f@#king asshole. Unless you want assholes, working for you and representing your business?
- ✓ They are sucking up to you. You're an essential pawn in their scheme. They want you to like them, respect them, BELIEVE them if it comes down to it. Suck Ups. NEVER trust them.

Like I said. It's f@#king challenging to identify a Schemer employee. Subterfuge. It's what they do. If you have someone in your business, which you can genuinely trust, get their take on things. What are the rumblings about your suspected Schemer around the office? Are they well-liked or secretly despised? Maybe contact ex-employees and find out what they have to say? (Do this with caution - the Schemer has a network of unwitting spies everywhere!).

This is where you know the Art of War, thanks to Sun Tzu and you've played many a good chess match in your time. Two can play this game, and you very cleverly can turn the tables, pull the proverbial rug out from your staff's so-called strategy play.

Sometimes you know, they know, you have the upper hand, notwithstanding that you are their f'in boss and then you have that hell yeah moment and fist pump or high five yourself.

Got you bitches!
Who's the tough one now aye?

The Schemer as Boss

The Schemer Boss may be in a position to be scheming, strategizing, thinking tactically, plotting next moves for the business and while there is nothing wrong with that if it is for productive professional reasons. Suppose it is just scheming for the sake of stirring up certain employees than that is 100% bullshit.

Really? What are you scheming about? If you're a Machiavellian Motherf@#ker around your own office, take a damn long hard look at yourself. Focus on the important shit, like hiring quality people, and leading them properly.

There's nothing good to say about the Schemer. They cause discord, destruction, and disengagement. In short, they're cancer. And what do you do with cancer? Cut it the f@#k out before it spreads. Go f@#k yourself if this is you. Truly.

The Umpire's Rule - 11% Stay | 89% Gone

Pyramid selling, the next best thing since sliced bread product salesman and the like is the Schemer's forte. They are always brewing up something. Whether it is to cut corners on production, find a way to slip out of doing something, scheming up things and then trying to bring team members on board the train.

This one needs to be reviewed as to what they are up to, what intel you can glean from others (careful they are not on their Scheme Team) and performance management of this one is iffy at best as unless you say something directly for them to cool their shit, then they are all but ready for their new adventure elsewhere.

THIS PAGE IS LEFT INTENTIONALLY BLANK

Why?

**Stay engaged because you must complete
the exercise to see if you have any of these
on the team. Heaven Forbid!**

THE BULLSHIT ARTIST

PULL THE OTHER LEG

bullshitartist
Your Workplace, Anywhere

⋮

08

BULLSHIT
ARTIST

08

65,377 views
bullshitartist yeah that was my idea #bullshitartist
View all 11,284 comments
8 AUGUST

PLAYER 08 - THE BULLSHIT ARTIST

The Bullshit Artist employee is a Schemer that is self-promoted. They are next level, so many stories to tell; they invented this, made that, they know that person, blah blah blah, but weaving in a good story of make-believe sprinkled with just a bit of reality to make it foolproof. Go back and read their resume to see for yourself.

The Bullshit Artist employee is one of those who blame others for their stuff-ups. They are playing the three cups game, but they told you the ball is under one of them. Lie. They are just up to no good and not being straight up. You don't know what to believe. They bullshit everything from their timesheet to their sales numbers, to the stocktake, to whatever they can get away with to show they are an invaluable productive team player when if you dig down just a bit and scrape some of that polish off; yep, there is a turd.

The Bullshit Artist employee, on the other hand, doesn't put much energy into anything, except:

✓ Firstly, when they say something, double-check if what they are saying is even true, as it is likely them just wanting to hear their own voice, and looking around to see who is tuning in.
✓ They are expert at grandstanding, oh yeah, I know him or her, partied with them, was out on their boat, is my sister's uncle's publicist or whatever bullshit they can just make up.
✓ Their resume should be a highly prized and well-sold template on how to fool your new employer with this

foolproof list of bullshit work stuff. Yep, we know the fool who took them on, right?

✓ Coming up with excuses as to why that might not work, bagging it as a crap idea and then if one does pay dividends, out comes the sneaky bullshit artist to remind you that in a meeting, oh so very long ago that was their idea.

✓ If they are in your sales department, then you have got a whole heck more trouble. You need to thoroughly check what deals they have written, even check on a few clients if all is okay with their contact with the Bullshit Artist.

✓ If they are supposed to be licensed or certified as a requirement for their role, then double-check that all is legit with the issuing authority. The Bullshit Artist knows how to use design editing programs, and his mate is a whizz at InDesign and churning out all sorts of professional certification, and the like. Just an add-on skill from their fake student ID days and perfected their craft to fool you.

Other characteristics of your Bullshit Artist are:

✓ They are master manipulators. If they are in sales, then just imagine what the f@#k they have offered clients/ customers to close deals. Not only the set of steak knives, right? Could be all sorts of stuff you don't want to become a compliance nightmare down the track, after they are long gone, and your credibility and more are on the line.

✓ Highly recommended is a mystery shopper to go in front of them so you can get honest feedback as to what was said to make a deal happen. This could be the worst crap you have to deal with, once these f@#ks are long gone, but your client comes at you saying here is the list of all the goodies I was promised. Yep, happens all too often.

✓ There appear to be lots of time off, or impromptu excuses to duck home early or need to go to the Doctor for something, when many times they may be moonlighting somewhere else, making some extra cash on the side or at the races. They might have even attended a funeral for their aunt, who has already passed away three previous times.

✓ Usually, they have another recognisable profile: The Schemer and there is overlap for this one that you just all too often find that they are in Sales.

✓ The Bullshit Artist's sneakiest thing is that they will keep straight-faced, not blink or break actor mode when they say that f@#k up was not caused by them but blame it on Peter in Customer Service. And they get away it. They are straight-up bullshitters deserving of the best actor award. No, a boot out the door is more appropriate.

✓ In the past, they really did attend an acting class because it is now just part of their disguise and almost like a Ventriloquist's doll meets Chucky where lips are moving, but is any of it real?

So, pay attention to who this person interacts with, in their role in the workplace as internal staff can help you figure out their game, or if they are client-facing then next-level recon, a mystery shopper is required. Their bullshit, like they went fishing and caught the biggest one in the lake and now the folks from Guinness World Records wants to interview them, just goes in one ear and out the other, but when served up in a professional capacity, deal-related, business on the line decisions just cannot be tolerated. They will be the demise of your business the moment it comes unstuck, and the customer comes for you.

The Bullshit Artist as Boss

The Bullshit Artist Boss is the employee version amplified. They have the authority of Boss sprinkled in, so now you have an ego, pompous attitude, a level of "Oh yeah aha, that's right bitch". Their stories are just as good. They may have bullshitted their way to promotion and cannot let the charade stop; otherwise, they will stand out like dogs' balls.

In fact, in the interview process for new salespeople to join the team, they probably did an outstanding job at bullshitting all the great amount of commission and bonus the person will make, selling x number of cars each month, just like Terry who made $300,000 last year or Steve who earned $80,000 selling software subscriptions all because of their outstanding leadership. So, the Bullshit Artist Boss is actually the judge who gives out the best actor awards. Even worse is when the Bullshit Artist Boss and his Bullshit Artist protégé team up, then God help us all as it's double jeopardy and time to close up shop and run for the hills.

The Umpire's Rule - 9% Stay | 91% Gone

What is real, and what is made up shit? The Bullshit Artist has just far too much crap, and frankly, they have graduated from the Schemer to next level, even you don't know what to believe. This one needs to be pinpointed directly to their work performance, KPIs, and overall production and team culture fit.

There is a slim chance that some attention and performance management could rewire them a little, but ultimately you will have to determine if their bullshit is just storytelling that goes in one ear out the other or ensure it does not mean a detriment to distraction to work overall. In all likelihood, these ones need to go.

THIS PAGE IS LEFT INTENTIONALLY BLANK

Why?

**Another pause, few more sips or even
a scull of your fine drink to allow you to adjust for a moment. Remain calm!**

THE BOSSY BRITCHES

GET BACK IN YOUR PLACE

bossybritches
Your Workplace, Anywhere

⋮

09

BOSSY
BRITCHES

09

158,007 views
bossybritches the boss said I'm in charge #bossybritches
View all 9,551 comments
9 SEPTEMBER

PLAYER 09 - THE BOSSY BRITCHES

The Bossy Britches employee is a toned-down version of the Control Freak, thankfully, but still bloody annoying. Either their years on the job or position or just attitude makes them want to be the centre of attention, have the last word and tell most of the staff what to do.

They are not just bossy, but also meddling in other areas, offering their version of help, via a, do it this way, my way is the right way approach.

On the other hand, the Bossy Britches employee doesn't put much energy into anything, except look busy, telling others to do the work which is pretty much work they should be doing and yet they are pissing people off along the way.

The Bossy Britches employee is:

✓ A hodge-podge of a few profiles all mashed up as they start off just lovely, Angel like and attempts to manipulate in getting things done their way.
✓ Promising other team members, they will do them a favour in return or just let them know how they can help in the future.
✓ This form of passive bossiness is their most favourite, so they think they are liked. If not getting their way, the aggressive side is released, and now we have a whole shitstorm brewing, or if you don't do that, this will happen, and it's your fault, so just do it now as I say.
✓ More often in management, empowered with this make-believe delegation pill that they just think it gives

them the authority to be a stick-wielding Sergeant Major and yet this is a civilian role.

✓ Supervisors are the worse kind as their bossiness helps them try and delegate away a lot of their own workload to others to make their life easier while using the cover of, they are busy looking after the team if they are ever called on it.

✓ The Bossy Britches is likely a long-time employee and knows the alarm code, how much water is used to refill the toilet tank, how much printer toner is used and more. I don't mean that verbatim. Yes, I am taking the piss. But they are so well-entrenched in the company, they know it all, and almost assume they are in the boss role.

✓ The Bossy Britches can possibly go through a reconditioning program to get them to tone done their bossy attitude and still retain some semblance of good supervising or manager type skills, without the sprinkle of shit, but that requires some training and supervision from yourself. Otherwise, they will just keep bossing people to have another sick day, or your good staff joins the revolving door of exits out of there.

Other characteristics of your Bossy Britches employee are:

✓ They know it all, been there, done that and might have worked in many areas of the business, which reinforces to them how much they know, so do it my way they say.

✓ They'll make excuses to cover their ass when a task was delegated to the team is not done, citing they told so and so to do it, so maybe they should speak to them first. Yes, they get snarky. They are trying to call your bluff. So, go and talk to the other person directly and listen to the 'he said she said' story for yourself. A great shapeshifter, the Bossy Britches is.

It's difficult for you if this person is a family member within the business as that requires almost sit down marriage style counselling to get them to agree to tone down their Bossy Britches attitude. Performance management with these ones can work for a limited time, and they will revert back once your eyes are off them and onto other lazy f@#ks to sort out.

The Bossy Britches as Boss

The Bossy Britches Boss is almost given a free pass in their profile with the exception of showing good leadership and concise instructions and directives, rather than be bossy in the sense of a busy body Bossy Britches. If there are elements of other profiles that the Boss carries then there is a real problem and depending on which profile mix, you either have an opportunity to correct it, or you are a f@#king powder keg ready to explode. Keep your shit in check and be the Good Boss okay mate?

The Umpire's Rule - 37% Stay | 63% Gone

This one is tricky. If the Bossy Britches is in a management or supervisor role, then it is essential to check if their bossiness is well-founded and part of their directives to the team. If it is just a power trip like the Control Freak, it needs to be corrected via some training.

However, if the Bossy Britches just likes to boss anyone around, in all sorts of manner, to get out of doing particular tasks or bossing people and they are just uncomfortable to be around and makes the culture unpleasant then this needs to be brought up in their performance review. Watch out they become all bossy with you, and you are just escalating them even more. This is skating on thin ice, so important to be well documented and managed.

THIS PAGE IS LEFT INTENTIONALLY BLANK

Why?

You have a few of those right? Well for sure the next one is a given. Don't laugh; these ones have cost you lots.

THE SICKIE

YOU'VE RUN OUT OF EXCUSES

FU **sickie**
Your Workplace, Anywhere

⋮

10

**THE
SICKIE**

10

190,915 views
sickie not feeling 100% and tomorrow's Friday #sickie
View all 18,694 comments
10 OCTOBER

PLAYER 10 - THE SICKIE

Being sick is par for the course as everyone at some point gets sick; we are all human. Some people are sick, while some are very sick, and that is genuine and acknowledged it's, unfortunately, a part of life we are all affected by at some point.

But the Sickie employee profiled here is the type that is sick on a Monday, cough or put on their sick voice when leaving their "I can't make it in today" message on voicemail, or a pattern of just bullshit excuses of being sick, one after another story of utter bullcrap.

They cannot make a full week of work without coming up with some excuse for being sick. It just drains on resources, others covering their workload, when they are miserable and just don't like their job. They make themselves fall ill because they want to avoid work.

But being sick means, you don't have to waste any annual leave entitlement and instead take a sick day and be paid to have a day off on a Friday or a Monday and make it a nice long weekend and woohoo it's now fun time. Oh, you can't have been that sick after all. Don't you think we noticed this shit? You posted your fun times on social media you dumb dumb.

The Sickie employee is a master manipulator. There is a habitual pattern from job to job, which never seems to come up in a reference check. The Sickie employee knows how to play the game so well, when their Doctor just writes them a note to take time off, so they don't have to listen to their dramatic, made up, sick story, which all too often they have heard it before.

The Sickie employee, on the other hand, doesn't put much energy into anything, except:

✓ They are the first to smell someone's perfume, air freshener, gosh even a fart in the office, complaining it is giving them a headache, and then escalate that throughout the day to provide them with a nice excuse to go early.

✓ They are great planners of their own events, incorporating in some post-recovery time, on your dime, after a great night out, yet if they are the planner of your events, it isn't very impressive, because they just don't give a toss. Anything outside of their typical work hours for you might upset their body clock, and that means they overslept the alarm and miss arriving on time, let alone showing up at all.

✓ Ask the payroll person often about how many sick days they have left to know that there planned long weekends are paid for and not infringe on their accrued holidays. Oh no, those are saved up for real-time off.

Other characteristics of your Sickie employee are:
✓ They are not always the first to get sick in the office. For example, if it is flu season and a couple of people are genuinely ill, then a few starter coughs from them during the week and oh no now they have the flu, and oh hello, it just happens to be Friday again. Well played.

✓ They are leaving a trail of Friday or Mondays or the day before their normal shift ends to score a three-day break. Check with their manager or HR on this pattern and open your eyes to the games they play with you and do something about it.

✓ Usually, they are the first to complain about hygiene in the workplace. People's food in the refrigerator contaminating their lunch or office refurbishment and fresh paint is a nasal nuisance and giving them a migraine.

✓ The most annoying part about the Sickie is that they are for the most part in good health but manifest up an illness or reason to go home and visit the Doctor to prove they went there and get sympathy and a protection of sorts that you won't go after them.

✓ They love the attention and solicit people's comments about how they feel and their genuine care towards them, and it just reinforces how credible their story is to themselves.

✓ It's difficult for you to do anything about it because you are just not quite sure if this is the one-time you call them out, that it is for real; however performance management does not help in this situation because all it will do is build up anxiety with them, they will turn on you because they feel under pressure, singled out, and of course guess what - they now feel sick. All because you started it. Move them on.

The Sickie as Boss

The Sickie Boss is a problem for the business and the team. Again, not talking about genuine sickness, health issues or even worse as that can cause all sorts of problems for a company, but where there is a behaviour of just being sick to avoid the workplace, underlines other issues that need to be dealt with immediately.

The Umpire's Rule - 6% Stay | 94% Gone

As stated before, put aside any real sickness of which you are compassionate about and find out if it is something that is real, not imaginary. If the cough is an excuse to get out of work, that shows the Sickie has escalated from the Lazy F@#K to get time off because they just don't want to be at work, and it is the one time they are actually sick; sick of work that is.

The Sickie needs to be tightly controlled via performance review, watching for even more sick days due to the undue pressure they will blame on you. Similarly, to showing an interest in their wellbeing as you do with the Moody F@#K and the Sooky Bubba, this one you must watch as the Sickie is playing you for a dumb dumb. At a certain level of you being taken down the proverbial garden path long enough, you should now go enough is enough and exit them.

THIS PAGE IS LEFT INTENTIONALLY BLANK

Why?

No matter where you are, a Library,
in a meeting studying this or in seat 2A let out a 4-letter
word starting with F. No!

YOU CAN'T TOUCH THIS

WATCH THIS SPACE

youcanttouchthis
Your Workplace, Anywhere

584,221 views

youcanttouchthis don't even try #youcanttouchthis

View all 63,947 comments

11 NOVEMBER

PLAYER 11 - THE YOU CAN'T TOUCH THIS

Take a Bully and watch them play you for a dumb dumb, that's the You Can't Touch This employee. Haha, they can't touch me. I do most of the work around here anyway.

The You Can't Touch This employee is a mashup of Bossy Britches, Control Freak, Bully, Lazy F@#K and bordering on the Devil. They think they have the Midas touch, that they are the hardest working employee and that the place wouldn't run so well without them.

They know their legal rights; they know their contract, and they have made themselves appear to be indispensable in the workplace.

The You Can't Touch This employee, has picked up the traits of the Bullshit Artist and Schemer employees, and this one is a real piece of work. They receive the award for being the player chameleon and should be in a magic show as they have so many tricks up their sleeve. It is a wonder they are still employed when really if you quantify their day and production and the contribution, it is a bittersweet f@#k all.

All too often you will hear the You Can't Touch This employee say, "Get someone else to do it", "Make them handle that", "I don't have time to be working on that small shit", "I'm helping run the company". They are in dreamland and need to be woken the f@#k up.

This is where you, as Boss will have to take your tough stance and power it up. These wannabe tough ones are now on fire, they are your next potential legal nightmare, and they are arming themselves up with anything to get to you. You need to get yourself prepared, be well informed, know all your legal options and protect yourself while preparing for your battle that they will not have seen coming. Do not underestimate these clever bastards.

The You Can't Touch This employee has a lot going for them and not in a positive way:

✓ Firstly, they should have the ringtone of MC Hammer's 'You Can't Touch This' song, because they strut around with an entitlement that they are the best.
✓ You speak, they listen. They are very good listeners. They are analysing what you say, listening for a congratulatory, complimentary, pat on the back nicety to reinforce their egos. If you can do that, you can add your request or directive for them to do something. They won't do it anyway but will delegate it to someone they have intimidated on the team to be their little bitch.
✓ They are the leader of the resistance, as they see it, and they know their workplace rights, have the local Office of Fair Work or similar in your country as a favourite speed dial in their phone. Likely, their sister is a lawyer, which everyone in the office has heard them spout many a time (even if she is a divorce lawyer with zero employment law practice experience). All designed to intimidate people from calling their bluff.
✓ This player is not a new employee by any means. They have clocked some time with the company and know it inside out, way better than the Bossy Britches. These ones are a strategist, to ensure that work gets done, they do little of it, but appear to be all over it, so the

155

good outcomes become their praise. Any issues, well they fall back on someone else that this person has so well placed in the line of fire.

Other characteristics of the You Can't Touch This employee is:

✓ They are Bossy Britches, Schemer, Bullshit Artist and Lazy F@#K moulded into one. They can move with precision in the workplace, appearing on all levels to be a superstar employee, yet look closer, talk to the team for those you know won't say a word back to them, and you will find there is no weak point for you to attack. If they were straight up as good as they are in playing the game where you can't touch them as they were in being a role model employee, then you would be at a whole next level of business success. Instead, they are scheming, planning, getting ready for their payday, whether you give them a pay rise because they said they deserve it, or you don't provide them with one, and they seek to extort it from you via other measures. Just exit these one's fast.

✓ Many of the team are intimidated by them yet hang out with them almost like a sense of nervous friendship, so they don't get bullied.

✓ These ones are building their network. It extends to employees, suppliers, service providers, etc. as they create their storyline of who they are in the business, and everyone is almost at this one's beck and call. It is a questioning time as to who is the boss here. They run the game on so many levels.

✓ Watch out for others that appear to be groomed by this player. They are building little mini-me's and amassing their army of those obedient to them when they need something done.

✓ The amount of crap they have caused for your business, you will likely never know, as they are masters at disguise, and nothing really points back to them. Sometimes it is a gut feeling, sometimes one of their following slips up and you get your piece of intel to validate aha it was you, you bastard. Nevertheless, anyone at the stage of You Can't Touch This should have only one final touch, and that is of a boot imprint on their ass as they are kicked out the door. Yes, I digress, they are formally, professionally, legally removed from the company like yesterday. No footprints allowed. Just saying.

✓ The more time they are given to roam freely without being hindered just encourages them to morph into the Devil and the transition time for them to do so is quick so save your business from this one now.

The You Can't Touch This as Boss

The You Can't Touch This Boss is a real problem especially if they have Bully and Control Freak added in their mix. They will step on toes, harass, bully, intimidate and overall be obnoxious, rude, arrogant, and so much more including that the place is a shithole to work in. All because of you!

You need to get yourself in order and that of your business pretty right damn quick smart before you have a mutiny, lawsuit or worse on your hands.

The Umpire's Rule - No Stay | 100% Gone

Gone, Get Out, History. The You Can't Touch This is part of the axis of evil employees, and they are not redeemable. They play a true cat and mouse game with you, and if you get sucked in and let your guard down, they will go back to their ways and you think all is calm again in the house, not a creature stirring not even a mouse.

Okay forget the rhyme, but what is lurking in your workplace 'house' is a monster that just does not give a shit. Your turn to scare them away, all professionally of course and with expert legal help. Hurry!

THIS PAGE IS LEFT INTENTIONALLY BLANK

Why?

We left this prick to last. We are nice with our words because they never are. Be firmly seated for this one and keep anything away from you that may cause harm. This next one, if on your team has done plenty. They are scum!

THE DEVIL

YOU CAN GO STRAIGHT TO HELL

devil
Your Workplace, Anywhere

⋮

12

12

666,666 views
devil let me tell you exactly how it's going down #devil
View all 666,666 comments
EVERY DAY

PLAYER 12 - THE DEVIL

Shit! F@#k! You've got the devil working for you. Let's not sugar coat it. This bitch or bastard doesn't give a flying f@#k about you, your authority, skill, etc. They are the one who is the workplace Hero, not you. They believe they're running the company, not you. Wake up!

They are the one who has read their employment contract front to back, back to front. They are so clever at doing enough to look busy, enough that you can't quite pull them up on their work, or have others tied around their finger to do their dirty work for them. It's at all levels.

These are either long-time employees who surpassed every other manager or boss and so well entrenched you need an iron-clad case to clear them out or one of those Jekyll and Hyde types - amazing actor in the interview process and right asshole after onboarding and cruisy days of training. It's that moment where you go "holy shit, how did I miss that?"

No, the Devil isn't another way of saying you have a bully in your midst. Not by a long shot. The Bully seeks to take their shit out on those around them. The Devil wants to take you down. Destroy you.

The Devil is created - they're not born. The Devil employee may very well have been your Angel employee that turned. Or your average, hard-working, happy enough, employee.

And then something happened.

Maybe that Lazy F@#K left them holding the bag one too many times.

Perhaps that f@#king Bully ripped them a new one (for no good reason) in front of someone they wanted to impress.

Or it could be that they're just sick of your shit.

Whatever the reason, it's your fault. You let the Lazy F@#K get away with it. You've not done anything to stop the Bully. And now they want to destroy you. Well, at least cause havoc for you and maybe 'earn' themselves a nice little payout. They want to make you pay.

The Devil employee is to be immediately exited. Easier said than done, but possible. But seriously this one is the worst shitbag of the team. They are many of the profiles wrapped up in one. They are a shapeshifter, a master manipulator. They are not able to be rewired.

Don't dare think a new role will work or try to put them on notice or a performance warning. They will shred you to pieces and take you down and sabotage the company if they know you are out for them.

This requires some Special Ops, get your shit all sorted, paperwork all lined up, legal counsel supporting you and whatever dollars it takes ever so nicely to boot their ass to the curb.

Exiting a Devil requires finesse and the right protocol to do it. It demands another strong person of seniority, management etc., to be present when moving on the Devil employee. An outside Consultant who the team may believe is there to help improve the process, or expansion plans (whatever story is needed) can be a good strong advocate for the Boss when dealing with exits like this one. If the company has security, then they best be put on standby, but don't give too much away in case security is mates with the Devil and they get a heads up what is about to go down. Not a good place to be in, so be careful with your moves.

Once the Devil employee breaks into full Spawn of Satan mode, you'll know it. Without a doubt. There are a few signs that a former Angel might be a Devil in disguise, though. Look out for things like:

✓ An increase in their average sick days.
✓ They are asking HR for a special chair because their back is a little sore.
✓ Large transfers of company data.
✓ Clockwatching where there was previously none. (they're pissed, so they're maintaining the persona for now, but they'll be damned if they give you an extra second of their time they don't need to).
✓ They exhibit every other player and cover the entire spectrum, causing havoc and mayhem and the cost to the business on so many levels is more than you will ever know.

If you think you have a fallen Angel in your midst. I've got some not so good news for you. It's going to hurt. Hell, hath no fury like an employee scorned. Not in this day and age anyway. We've got some suggestions for you -

basically, you need to rip off that band-aid. They have got to go and go now!

The Devil as Boss

The Devil Boss is an automatic reason to resign. People are intimidated, scared, bullied, harassed, and this is not a Devil Wears Prada movie or Gordon Ramsay Hell's Kitchen episode, the Devil Boss is a toxic person who has no business being a boss.

If you are the Devil Boss, then seek help immediately and see if there is any possibility of changing your ways, unlikely as it is. Otherwise, there is only one place you are going, and you will likely take the business with it. The End. It is the end of the road if this is you.

The Umpire's Rule - No F@#King way they stay | 100% Gone

There is nothing to discuss. The Devil goes straight to Hell. You better have a damn good employment contract that you can leverage, yet this requires special ops to be called in with expert legal advice to run through all your options and have everything triple checked.

If all else fails with firing them legally of course, then look seriously at redundancy, regardless of the payout amount. Get the dollars from somewhere and even readjust that role (outsource or whatever you can do so not seen as to then just replacing them and get yourself into more hot water).

See those dollars as an investment into fixing the workplace, God knows how many sales lost, or purposeful f@#kups were made that you cannot quantify but if you did it would be a heap more than getting rid of this scumbag. Employment legal advice and assistance from the experts is your only friend here and is an absolute necessity. Do not overlook it whatsoever.

Nothing to say except watch your back and get them the F out of the workplace. There is no redeemable quality whatsoever with the Devil. This is urgent AF!

THIS PAGE IS LEFT INTENTIONALLY BLANK

It's pretty darn obvious why.

How does the list look? How polluted
is your workplace? Just think for a moment how much more
business, fewer headaches, better team culture you will
have when you deal to these 'players' because that's exactly
what they are. And if you are any of these,
then fix yourself up ASAP!

NOW REALLY GET FIRED UP

If you've done the work and been ruthlessly honest about your employees and your shortcomings, by now, you know who the Lazy F@#K in your office is and are on the alert for any Angels who have turned!

But some of you may need a little more convincing. Let's give you some real-life examples of how some of these players affect, control, manipulate, destroy your business, and if this doesn't get you Fired Up, to do something, then nothing will. Game over!

Stories from The Trenches: Here comes 'The Angel'

Remember when I said it was all your fault? In the case of the Angel, it truly is. Angel employees aren't a threat to your business (unless of course, they turn) however it's the Angel Boss that's the real problem.

Jack was the Owner & Managing Director of a successful and rapidly expanding manufacturing business (let's call it Good Vibes). Jack often sat in on staff interviews and was always involved in some way in hiring staff. He liked to think of himself as an empathetic people person and a reasonably good judge of character. He was a fairly good judge of character.

Good Vibes was a pleasant place to work. The culture was open. Work got done, but fun was had. Jack was a good leader (some might say, an Angel!). As well as salaries on the higher end of the curve, he rewarded staff with spontaneous lunches and fun team events. Working hours were flexible (within reason), and people came to work happy and left the same way.

Just as importantly for staff morale, his 'door was always open'. Most of the time, this meant employees were comfortable enough to approach him about any problems or mistakes that occurred. Sometimes staff would approach him with personal or personnel issues. He handled these with the appropriate amount of diplomacy and care - and was sure to get his trusted HR Manager, Maria, involved. Jack believed the organisation's success and rapid growth had a lot to do with the successful company culture. His employees were treated well and happy, and so were his customers.

Hot damn! Good Vibes sounds like a great place to work, doesn't it? Almost too good to be true! The truth is, Jack, being the empathetic Angel, he was, had put a tremendous amount of thought and effort into getting the company culture right. Great job, Jack!

Both the Sales and Service teams had grown rapidly, in line with expanding his customer base. He'd promoted Joanna to oversee the Service team. He always promoted internally wherever possible. He had a few superstars on his Sales team and 2 of them, Samantha and Andrew had applied to be promoted to the Sales Team Manager. But they were not quite right or ready to oversee the entire team.

It was proving difficult to find the right fit, so when Susan walked into Maria's office for an interview, she was the answer to everyone's prayers! Susan had previous experience within the industry, and Jack felt they were on the same wavelength when it came to sales philosophy. Jack passionately explained his strong aversion to pushy sales tactics. He believed a great product; superb service and a responsive sales team suited his business best. Susan concurred.

Because Susan was moving to the area, her existing employer knew she was leaving as soon as she secured a job. Maria received a glowing report from them - confirming what she and Jack already thought! Yes, Susan always met or exceeded team sales targets. Yes, it's true; she was a very supportive leader. Sure, they'd hire her again. Maria was having trouble getting hold of her other referee (a previous employer). Jack told her not to bother with the additional reference, and this was all they needed!

Jack put aside 30 minutes to talk separately with both of his unsuccessful internal applicants, Samantha, and Andrew, before announcing Susan was joining Good Vibes. Delivering bad news wasn't his favourite task; however, he was very clear about why the decisions had been made. Although they were both visibly disappointed, he knew they left his office with their morale intact and a good plan for their development within the organisation. He even allowed himself to feel a smidge of smugness about how well it had all gone down.

After her company induction, Jack and Susan had a great discussion about the Sales team and its vision. He enlisted her to help with Samantha and Andrew's succession plan, explaining that they were both keen to grow within the sales team, and had applied for her job. He assured her they weren't harbouring any grudges about her appointment.

Susan jumped in, all guns blazing. In her first team meeting, she had them all wear name stickers. She went around the room, asking them to all stand-up and share their lowest sales month numbers. They felt it was a little odd, but nothing to worry about.

When the Sales team arrived the next day, they found their usual workstation rearranged. Half on one side of the room, half on the other. Susan explained that anyone whose lowest month was 50% or more below target would be sitting together on the room's far side. This was to motivate them. Once they made up for it by reaching 50% or more above the target, they'd be moved to the other side.

Samantha, who had consistently outperformed everyone on the team for the last six months, had a very rough few months sales-wise, when she first joined Good Vibes. Her desk had been moved to the far side of the room. In fact, she was right at the very back, right beside the photocopy room. She was a little taken aback but decided to put it down to Susan's unique approach to motivation. Perhaps she could learn a thing or two from her. Besides, she knew she was on target for her best sales month ever, so she'd be out of there in no time.

She was a little worried about some of the other Sales team members, though. She'd been working with Sean to help him improve his closing technique. He'd been improving. Both Samantha and Jack believed he was the right fit for the Good Vibes sales team. Not overly pushy at all, great with clients, he just needed to work on objections and resilience a little more.

Sean was on the 'other' side with her and was sitting quietly at his desk, staring into space. As the 'mother' of the team, Samantha made a point of having a quick pep talk with each of her fellow 'other side' crew. She didn't want them to lose heart.

Andrew was feeling weird. He knew Samantha didn't deserve to be singled out - and he knew her figures were always better than his. On the other hand, he was on the good side. Where he intended to remain. Now felt like a good time to get on side with their new boss, so he casually asked if she'd like a coffee as he walked by her office to the kitchen. She was delighted and gave him her order with a lovely smile.

Jack had met a potentially big customer for Good Vibe at a conference. They had finally made contact, and he asked Samantha to sit in on the conference call with him, as she would take over the account if they won it.

The meeting went well. As she left Jack's office, Samantha mentioned Susan's unique motivation techniques. Jack was concerned that they weren't in line with the Good Vibes culture he'd worked so hard to grow. He felt uneasy, and there was a tiny voice in his head telling him no apparently 'supportive' Manager would use any technique like that to motivate their staff. He chose to ignore it. He really did click with Susan and wanted to give her a chance to understand the company culture.

Susan seemed to take his request to stop her unique motivation experiment quite well. She confirmed it had worked 'brilliantly' for her in the past but understood if he 'wasn't ready for such state-of-the-art techniques'. She also mentioned, very casually, that Samantha appeared very disgruntled about missing out on the promotion, and that she'd seemed unwilling to help when she'd asked to find a particular folder on the server. It didn't sound like the Samantha that Jack knew, he wondered if she was more disappointed than he knew. He decided to keep a close eye on the situation.

Susan was visibly angry when she returned to the Sales office. She slammed her office door and smouldered at her computer. After a few minutes, she opened her door and seemed to be over it. Her sneaky f@#king game face was on.

Just as Samantha was finishing her last sales call for the day, Susan sent her an email requesting she sends her an itemised breakdown of the sales for each of her accounts before leaving for the day. She had an appointment after work but felt she had no choice but to cancel it. She didn't want to risk upsetting Susan any further today, as she seemed very volatile. By the time she'd finished, it was just she and Susan left in the entire office. She felt oddly anxious. Since when did people feel anxious at Good Vibes?

She hit send on the email and began to pack up. Susan opened her office door and walked toward her. She didn't hold back. How f@#king dare she complains to Jack about her! What the f@#k made her think she knew anything about leading a sales team? She was a useless waste of space, and

Susan would make her life a misery until she left. With that, she turned on her heel and left. Susan was shaking and bewildered. She couldn't believe what had happened.

There was no one else around to witness what happened. No one will believe her anyway.

After a sleepless night, Samantha made an appointment with Maria and told her what had happened the previous night. Maria was oddly formal. She took notes and made the right noises, but she was much more guarded than usual.

Samantha didn't know that Susan had already been making the case around the business that she was uncooperative because she had been passed over for the promotion. With no witnesses, and Susan's outright denial of the claims, Samantha was ultimately told to stop making trouble, and Jack began avoiding her.

The vibes were rapidly becoming negative at Good Vibes.

What the F@#K went wrong?

It's tempting to focus on the behaviour of the Bully. Yes, Susan is a classic Bully. But we're talking about the Angel at the moment. In this case, the Angel Boss. But don't worry, Susan's time will come.

I get so frustrated when I hear cases like this. Jack built something truly f@#king great at Good Vibes. He was a benevolent boss without being a walkover. In other words, he was a well-balanced Angel Boss. He had done everything right. Right up until he hired f@#king Susan.

That's the problem with the Angel Boss. Things work great when they're dealing with reasonable human beings. But the Angel Boss is like catnip for sociopaths, like the Bully and the Schemer, and the Angel Boss is inherently too trusting and believes in the goodness of all humanity. And sociopaths know how to twist them around their little fingers.

If you're an Angel Boss, here is what your fellow Angel Jack did wrong, specifically.

✓ He told Susan what he wanted to hear during the interview, and then he let her simply agree with him.
✓ He believed his bullshit. Because he's proven what a good judge of character he was in the past, he considered Susan's first impression was a true and correct impression of her. When signs pointed toward Susan being a f@#king asshole, he chose to continue his original, more convenient and ego-boosting narrative.
✓ He didn't get a second referee for Susan or do his best due diligence. Again, his belief in his instincts, together with his rush to get the position filled caused him to circumvent the system he'd put in place. It's very likely that an existing employer might have said anything anyway to get rid of that f@#king bitch Susan. A previous employer might just take pleasure in telling it like it is, albeit they are few and far between due to privacy.
✓ He didn't trust his gut.
✓ He let himself be subtly manipulated.

✓ He didn't dig deep enough. He could easily have reserved judgement (especially since Samantha was a long-standing, well-trusted employee with an unblemished record) and found a way to check up on Susan subtly.

✓ He chose to ignore the situation (specifically ignore Samantha) as it was much more convenient not to think he'd just hired a problem.

If you're an Angel Boss, who's let some Susan type run roughshod over your staff and your business, really, you're pretty f@#ked. This is an extreme example of what can happen when the Angel Boss inside you isn't kept on a leash. Your need to be liked, admired - even adored! - by your staff and that is a problem. It's preventing you from behaving assertively when required, and as a result, your team, and your business will suffer.

Back to the story. Jack let this shit go on way too long. And by the time he had to admit to himself that Susan was poisoning his culture, it was too late to cut her loose without issues.

Rather than deal with the issue head-on, he chose to tippy-toe around it (that f@#king bitch Susan) for another year. Eventually, after losing half of his long-standing employees, he had to take action. He'd let too much bad shit be swept under the carpet to be able to performance manage her out, so he had no choice but to make her position redundant, and now he oversees the team.

Susan received a whopping payout, and even let loose on Jack as she walked out the door. Susan did fine, and she's currently spreading her toxic attitude at another business.

Good Vibes is slowly recovering. But it will never be quite the same. Neither will Jack.

Stories from The Trenches: It's 'The Devil'

Remember Samantha? She worked at Good Vibes and was on track to be their highest performing salesperson ever until Jack, her Angel Boss, employed that f@#king Bully Susan. Unbelievably, she still works there!

Samantha is very much an Angel employee (even able to pump out high achieving sales figures). She has an extremely long wick. She is empathetic and very attuned to the needs of others. And she's wonderfully optimistic - sometimes annoyingly so.

Susan continued to bully Samantha for the next few months until she got her boot out the door. The bullying was intermittent, though, and hard to predict. Throughout this period, Samantha remained optimistic. She was loyal to Good Vibes and Jack. It did hurt a little that her previously friendly and mutually respectful relationship with him appeared to have petered out. Or maybe she just imagined it. Jack was a busy man with lots of staff and a high turnover business.

She wondered to herself if she could have handled the whole Susan situation differently. Was she just being oversensitive?

Maybe she was, unconsciously trying to undermine Susan. Perhaps she was useless like Susan said.

She knew that Susan was bullying Sean too. And as was the case with her, there were never any witnesses to it. Sean confided in her, one evening after a particularly dreadful encounter. With Sean, Susan's tactic was mostly outright degradation and humiliation.

But sometimes she was more subtle and insidious - that day, she'd ordered him to fetch her lunch. He'd become increasingly anxious around her - and in general. As soon as he entered her office, his armpits started sweating big time. Within seconds, that area of his shirt was soaked.

Thus, the perfect opportunity for a Bully had fallen into Susan's lap. Initially, she sniffed a little and asked, "What's that smell?" Sean knew he didn't smell. He took a lot of care with his hygiene. Besides, his girlfriend would have told him if he smelled.

After she'd given her ridiculously particular lunch order (she'd made him write it down), Susan told Sean she'd had a complaint about body odour. Scratch that, she had 'several' complaints. She went on to give him a thorough explanation of hygiene and personal grooming. He felt so embarrassed and began to doubt what he knew to be true.

Susan, f@#k you. You evil bitch. Can't wait until you get what you deserve. Of course, he thought but did not utter those words.

Sean wasn't as resilient, nor as optimistic as Samantha. He didn't quite believe in all humans' intrinsic goodness as Samantha did, and he had less self-esteem than the others. She encouraged him to speak with Maria about it, but he received similar treatment to her, so every way you looked at it, it was a clusterf@#k.

She couldn't understand why Susan - a newcomer was being given the benefit of the doubt all the time. She felt hurt, and the injustice, when she thought about it too much made her throat constrict and her eyes water. She started to think about it all the time.

Meanwhile, Samantha's exterior world appeared unchanged. She continued to perform well (although one-month Andrew had outperformed her, which was unexpected) and she maintained her happy, supportive presence around the office. In the beginning, she'd awake each morning with the desire to have a great day. Then she'd settle for just an average day.

And before long, she just hoped for a day when Susan wasn't in the office. Sean eventually resigned. To be precise, he just didn't turn up one day.

This story is true, names changed of course, but show you the level of drama that can go on in the workplace and this is one of the milder ones shared from our research of various companies. We didn't want to share some really nasty ones just because some of the circumstances may reverse engineer back to a company or person. Then we have the Devil on our ass.

Although we certainly would know how to deal with them if they did come calling. Nevertheless, there is a lot of shit going on right now, either under a Bosses nose and avoiding it out of fear, laziness, weak leadership or likely have no clue it is even occurring.

WHERE'S EVERYONE AT?

By now, you will have assigned individual employees to a 'Player Profile' and be able to see how they either dominate, play games, are on cruise control or in the limelight, to name a few. Use this style matrix to see where everyone's at. Some are, of course, moving in and out of each quadrant, those sneaky one's playing a full field game. You have wised up and now know who they are and what needs to be done. Step up and take the trash out.

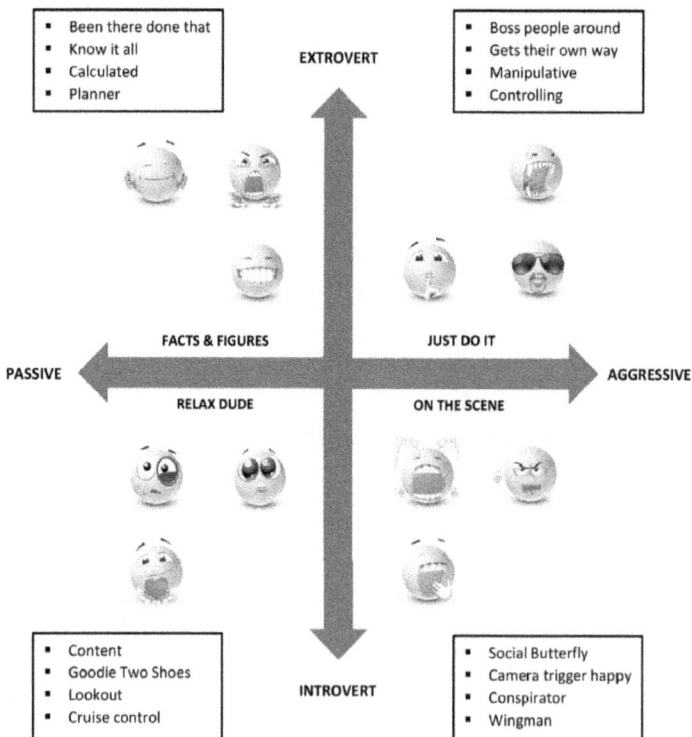

• Been there done that • Know it all • Calculated • Planner	• Boss people around • Gets their own way • Manipulative • Controlling

EXTROVERT

FACTS & FIGURES   JUST DO IT

PASSIVE ← → AGGRESSIVE

RELAX DUDE   ON THE SCENE

INTROVERT

• Content • Goodie Two Shoes • Lookout • Cruise control	• Social Butterfly • Camera trigger happy • Conspirator • Wingman

THIS PAGE IS LEFT INTENTIONALLY BLANK

Why?

**It's that purposeful pause just
to take a couple of deep breaths, clench
and release those fists and here we go!**

QUALITY CHECK VS. HOLY HECK

The list of performance measurements you will have for your business will be simple to complex, yet here are some key ones to doublecheck you cover these in your performance reviews. Small companies often have little to no performance review process let alone regularly scheduled reviews, yet this one major area of the business - people - the employees are such a significant engine powering up the company or sucking the lifeblood out of it, requires a lot of attention.

Performance reviews, evaluations, action plans, training are all necessities to keeping you and staff in check, accountable for their role and responsibilities and achieve what is required of them.

This was made clear in the hiring process, documented in their employment contract, reminded of daily as a team, reinforced in meetings and then if all becomes a futile exercise in trying to appease an employee's zero care factor then it becomes a well-documented catalyst for moving them on.

Some key performance review outcomes are:

Their **work output** is of high quality, and they have high standards, focused and attention to detail, accurate, procedure-driven **vs.** lots of errors, incomplete in their tasks and low-quality work with no real attention to detail.

You can **count on them** to be on time, reliable and dependable, follow process, directives and obey rules **vs.**

they have lots of time off, are unreliable, and have such a care-free work attitude like they just don't give a toss.

They are a **team player** who helps others, takes feedback seriously and are keen to learn to improve themselves and their contribution **vs.** isolating themselves if they can, not wanting to be involved in the team and it is evident, pushes back on any feedback or coaching and see it as criticism or picking on them.

Their **ability in the role** to be competent, be productive, complete assignments, tasks, follow instructions with a high level of competence and technical skills **vs.** they don't seem to have a grasp on the tasks in hand, miss deadlines, uncompleted projects with no sense of urgency and there is this lingering feeling of whether they are even competent or just playing lazy games.

They have a **productive output** and work ethic to get things done. They are busy, working to put in a good day's effort for a good day's pay and help the team be productive and deliver high-quality work **vs.** watching the clock for the next break, just going with the flow and no demonstratable effort they are productive whatsoever. They are more focused on putting in the hours then the output of work.

Have a **level of motivation** that is positive, it is good team spirit, a sense of pride in their work and is easily motivated, motivate others in-turn because of their desire to get things done **vs.** any lack of interest in being positive, boost team morale, show any signs of motivation, almost don't want to be there.

They are a **good decision maker** and as it pertains to their role they know what needs to be done, can make good business judgement and assessment of what is right and for the good of the company **vs.** not wanting to make an effort to use good common sense and judgement and rely on others to keep telling them what to do, a real disinterest in being self-sufficient when it comes to handling their role and responsibilities instead it's like they are being babied all the time.

Their **behaviour is good** from the way they dress, whether uniform or stated work attire, to their personal hygiene, language and how they act professionally, friendly and get along with the team **vs.** bending the rules on dress code and they are unclean, offensive, abrasive in communication and just an outright look at me, I don't give a shit how I dress and act in the workplace.

Get your performance review structure in place if not already.

Ensure you have regularly scheduled and conducted meetings to review performance.

Everything is documented, so you can review it each time you meet, or if you need it to exit someone, the trail will show effort, intent, action to assist this person who doesn't want to work but collect a paycheck. So, cover your ass.

WHY BOTHER WITH A PERFORMANCE REVIEW?

You know that people are at the core of your business to help make things happen, move product, drive sales, delighting customers and keeping the doors open for business.

Yes, we know the importance of positive and productive people within the workplace, and this guide has given you much intel to be able to tell if you have a good company culture and the environment in the first place and then secondly to identify those in your team that are a perfect fit to all of that and those who are on notice to shape up or ship out.

So, it is important, that the leadership team have a thorough and ongoing focus to help their employees grow, to learn, and create a great team environment, to own their roles, to want to come to work and they feel good, and thus it should come as no surprise to anyone that conducting performance reviews with each of their staff is par for the course.

Right from the get-go, when a new employee joins the team, they know that they will be evaluated. It is part of the interview discussion, stated in the employment contract and reminded again in the onboarding. Both parties understand and agree to it. There is no surprise, and it should be very clear; otherwise, you are leaving the door open to all sorts of hurt.

The message of a performance review is to help the business be successful, to ensure each team member is at their highest and best use and working in tandem to make the place better, to be successful and everyone to share in that success and have pride in their work and so forth. It is to be conveyed that these reviews are not designed to be disciplinary but to be a positive, focused meeting and assessment, so all are productive and positively driven and have the company's support to excel in their role.

So, let's get a few steps sorted.

1. Clearly laid out process.

As already touched on, the company and its managers must communicate the review process procedure and the expectations of what, why, how, when, etc. of the reviews are handled. It is written and communicated, a part of the onboarding process and scheduled. All parties acknowledge such, so there is no confusion or surprises to either party.

2. It's not a personal attack but is professional.

The review will look at several key measurements and include behaviours, actions, room for improvement, concerns, and more related to the employee's role, not as a personal attack. It is a fine line when tackling this area and how we say things can be interpreted in a whole different context, so it is important to be professional, not personal but still to the point.

3. Not just your way.

When reviewing the employees' actions on performing a certain task, be mindful that you have your way of doing things, it may or may not be how they were onboarded and trained in the role. Over time they may have found, improved, or invented a different way than what you expect, but maybe achieving the same or better outcomes. That initiative may be useful and should be discussed and acknowledged rather than a straight assumption that they are not following rules and procedures. So, double-check before firing off on this one. If it is blatant lack of care for the process, understand why they are not following protocol. This will be a telling moment as to whether the process needs adjusting or they need it.

4. Be clear and concise.

What is discussed in the performance review must be direct, factual, clear and to the point and from that an action plan can be created, one that has tasks or milestones of achievement that both parties are in agreeance with. This is a time to partner to make it work and get buy-in that the employee agrees with and make any changes or corrections and not just nod their head to keep the meeting moving quickly to the end.

5. Feedback to foster good outcomes.

Many times, feedback can be construed as negative in the context of delivery, such as you missed your production target last month and this is not good enough, versus the target for last month was 500 that we set in our previous action plan and you delivered 380, quite a significant shortfall from the target. Share with me why you think that happened?

Be more consultative to understand from their perspective and whether there were valid reasons such as machine broke down, time off sick, other factors work related out of their control but possibly within yours, or they are just not into it. This way, you can craft your feedback, assessment, and performance language appropriately, so it is professional and not construed as a personal attack. Remember?

This way, you could offer your expertise, advice, ways of improving the situation, additional training, etc., so they are a part of it, not just about getting smashed. If they are not engaged and pretty much checked out, you still go through the review formalities, take notes, work on an action plan, and so forth, knowing that the next meeting they are gone. No passengers are allowed.

Managers play a critical role in understanding their employees' career goals and crafting development opportunities to help their reports achieve their goals.

Conversely, where there is some great work, stellar performance, exceeding targets, positive feedback from others in the team regarding their contribution, ideas, and initiatives, and praise and recognition are given.

That boost in the spirit can do wonders for the workplace environment and their production. If it results in a bonus, or commission or some other appreciation that they value, goes a long way to building a harmonious workplace and not a combat zone.

6. Review and measure.

Each review is provided to the employee to keep track of the action plan and the next scheduled review. And of course, a copy is retained by management to refer to at regular intervals before the following planned review to see how they are progressing rather than waiting for next month, quarter or even annually and there is a WTF moment.

Yes, this is all pretty straightforward, yet many employers don't make time for this valuable component of managing their people, and yet that is an important engine to the business so why not make sure it is fine-tuned, well serviced and looked after so it looks after you.

Here is a flow for you to run through. It's one you can do with each employee you identified such as the Angel, the Lazy F@#K, the Moody F@#K, the Sooky Bubba and the Bossy Britches primarily to see if they are keepers or move them on.

Use it in conjunction with your performance reviews, issues, complaints, staff feedback, management statements and the likes to have a clear determination, and that is, either:

1. This employee is a valuable asset to the business and redeemable, and we can work together, through a structured approach to ensure they perform per the role,

responsibilities, duties, KPIs, performance and team player attitude etc. that I expect.

or

2. I have zero interest in allowing them to drag down my company any further, bully staff, cost me who knows how many sales because of their shit work ethic and their 'could not give a crap' attitude about work. They get zero of my time or my staffs. No third or fourth chances, they are history.

For our other players that you have unfortunately got in your midst such as the Control Freak, the Bully, the Schemer, the Bullshit Artist, the Sickie, the You Can't Touch This and of course the Devil, and these ones go straight out the door as quickly as you can and make sure you have that Employment Relations Legal support to do so.

You need to cover your ass and that of the business, big time.

Just to repeat, so please take notice. You need to cover your ass and that of your business big time. And you need to have experts in employment law helping you, especially with the nasty stuff that we have covered!

Now go through the flow.

GET FIRED UP FLOW - OR IT IS TIME TO GO

IDENTIFIED THEIR PROFILE?

Y — N → RESEARCH AND ASSESS

DO YOU REALLY HAVE A PERFECT 100% TEAM?

Y — N

DOES THIS PERSON EXHIBIT A DOMINANT PROFILE?

Y — N → IDENTIFY THEIR DOMINANT PROFILE AND START THERE

CONGRATULATIONS YOU ARE IN THE TOP 1% OF THE LUCKY BOSSES GROUP GLOBALLY OR DREAMING

DO YOU KNOW IF THIS PERSON IS COACHABLE AND THEY ARE PRODUCTIVE?

Y — N

NOW GO WRITE A HOW TO GUIDE TO CREATING THE MOST HARMONIOUS WORKPLACE AND HIRING REALLY NICE PEOPLE. ON SECOND THOUGHT, THAT'S MY NEXT BOOK IN THE MAKING NOW LOL 😊

BRAVO! KEEP UP REGULAR REVIEWS

DO YOU CONSIDER THEM AN ASSET/VALUABLE TO THE BUSINESS?

Y — N → REMOVE THEM FROM YOUR COMPANY NOW

N — Y

IS THERE SOMEONE ELSE ON THE TEAM OR IF YOU HIRE WILL THEY PERFORM THE ROLE MUCH BETTER?

IS THERE A NEW PRODUCTIVE PERSON AND THAT PROFILE IS HISTORY?

Y — N

DO YOU WANT TO SPEND TIME WORKING WITH THEM TO CORRECT THEIR BEHAVIOUR AND/OR PERFORMANCE?

MONITOR REGULARLY

REPLACE INTERNALLY OR SEARCH AND RECRUIT OR OUTSOURCE THE ROLE IF MORE MANAGEABLE

CREATE A 60-DAY PLAN TO EVALUATE NEXT 31-60 DAYS & THEN 61-90 DAYS

Y — N

N — Y

DO YOU HAVE SOMEONE ON THE TEAM THAT CAN TRAIN/COACH PROPERLY? OR DO YOU HAVE $ TO HIRE SOMEONE TO TRAIN? WILL THIS HELP YOU?

HAS THE TRAINING HELPED? HAS THIS PERSON NOW CORRECTED THEIR BEHAVIOUR AND PERFORMANCE IN LINE WITH THE ACTION PLAN AND DO YOU SEE A POSITIVE CHANGE?

Y — N

CREATE A 30-DAY ACTION PLAN AND IMPLEMENT TRAINING WHILE REVIEWING AGAINST AN AGREED PERFORMANCE PLAN

NOW WE ARE AT THE POINTY END - IT'S LEGAL TIME

You have gone through the motions. You've had a good read through this guide. You may have used plenty of expletives as I have throughout to emphasise your own rude awakening, shocking discovery or realisation that you are the cause of your company culture and then some. I do hope it's not the case and just a few employees that you can right royally get sorted and bring back your business from the brink of shithole status to where everyone wants to work, including you, and it is highly successful.

If you have determined you are the root cause of many of your company culture issues, take it upon yourself to swiftly get it sorted. Get your senior management, those in your implicit trust circle, to help change the workplace environment while you move fast and with sincerity to fix you.

If you have employees to deal with, then I recommend you have that meeting very quickly with your Head of Human Resources if you have one and discuss exactly your directive that this person or these people are removed and the best, legal and most professional way to do it. If it means that your performance reviews and warnings etc. are on file and give you your rights as an employer to do what you have to and there are no legal repercussions, you know what to do.

Suppose you have no such person within the organisation that handles the Human Resource side of things. In that case, I recommend you retain a company specialising in Employment Relations and legal advice and the support to carry things through.

Even if you have staff that handle these matters, I suggest you consult with such an external agency regardless, so you ensure you have everything sorted. This is going to become a tangled mess that could financially eat into your business. There is most certainly going to be a cost to make this person redundant (if you can - ask your legal team), yet the quickest and swiftest way by far otherwise the whole process of performance management and warnings is just going to antagonise majority of the players we have outlined herein that this has to be done as fast as possible.

These employment relations services are far better than a standalone lawyer who specialises in employment law as typically for a fee they will help you write a severance letter (which is templated anyway), and some advice they give is mostly cautious advice because what you are doing, is for most a little too aggressive for them. They just like to fill in templated letters for you and charge through the roof.

In our research, we have found all too often that the advice given was to sit down and talk with the employee, air your grievances and work things out. That was an utter waste of our time and predictable so much that some of these very professionals we were looking for guidance and advice from, immediately catapulted themselves to the lazy f@#k category and weren't on our payroll thankfully.

So, the reason and recommendation to check out Employment Relation type services are that they have a very effective framework in place where they can consult with you to get an overview of the company, discuss in detail in the strictest confidence as to your concerns for each employee you wish to either help through performance management because you see something in them that is a keeper or guidance to kick the others to the curb.

And this process can assist with implementing a performance management program for the company, all the support, templates, procedures to follow, including real help not just here, is the email with instructions saying you are on your own, good luck. Not the case at all.

They have a team of lawyers and specialists in employment law, and they have handled many cases, mediations, court appearances for employers, helping prepare for performance reviews, assisting with terminations including being present at meetings and ensuring everything is documented and run professionally and by the book. It absolutely has to be.

Do your search and find these companies and check them out. Some have memberships that enable you to incorporate them into your company way of doing business and can expand to employee onboarding, performance management, recognition programs, and more depending on how expansive their services are. Many want to help the employees as much as the employer too, to create that fair place to work and one that is free from a toxic culture or one rogue employee that upsets everything.

Yes...

- ✓ It comes at a cost.
- ✓ You should be able to write it off as a business expense. Check with your Accountant.
- ✓ Redundancy is not cheap, but work out how much business you lost, then compare it.
- ✓ You are going to be called everything under the sun - too bad. This is business. Yours.
- ✓ The scorned employee will likely take it all the way legally, so have that other company to back you up.
- ✓ It will feel so bloody well satisfying when you see a complete work environment shift to positive and that uplift in the team spirit.
- ✓ I will happily have a drink or two with you to celebrate that you got Fired Up!

THE GRACEFUL EXIT?

You've sought legal advice as it relates to employment matters. Right? You're not winging it or thinking you know what you are doing? The professional advice you seek is for a whole host of reasons, and unofficially obviously it is to CYA (yes cover your ass) because you are potentially going up against something worse than a competitor or a fierce marketplace, but soon to be ex-employee scorned.

Most of the time you will be advised to conduct a performance review, give the employee the opportunity to change their ways or better still for them to masquerade now as a good employee where you now have no clue if they are sincere or just treading water with you.

As you can reasonably expect, those regular meetings, which of course you made notes may assist strongly with your performance meetings and subsequent warnings if you decide to go this route, then you best ensure you have the full support of your HR team or an external employment law service to support you through the process as it is not going to be an easy one.

If you are given the green light to go straight in for redundancy, with the mindset of outsourcing the role or eliminating it entirely and with little to no notice required, depending on your country, state, and local requirements, then get it done.

Do not wait until the end of the day. Forget the bullshit some HR managers will tell you such as oh wait until payday, wait until closing time or end of their shift. No shut up, none of that is relevant. There is no time like the present. Do it now! No more excuses! No more delays!

You do not need to carry this person one more hour, let alone one more minute.

Have a trusted colleague be present as a witness to your professional conduct during the exit. Many employment services will provide you with the checklist, templates, and personal guidance through the entire process. It is very delicate, and it is just as much the soon to be ex-employees' livelihood as it is yours. But in this instance, the good for your company and the decision you have made ranks first and foremost. Just ensure you do not try and wing this and follow your professional advisers' guidance because it will most certainly heat up.

Do not be emotional. It's likely to be.
Do not apologise either. Just don't do it, bite your tongue.
Do not say sorry ever. There is nothing to be sorry for, other than you should have done this sooner. So sssh, no sorry whatsoever. If it is a common word for you like um, then just for this important mission, do not utter it.

You must stick to the facts. The truth shall set you free. Oh okay. But just facts matter.

Do not belittle, pick on, or be unprofessional. There is no need for it, and it is just putting you in a whole lot of hot water if you do, so keep it to yourself and bloody well shut up and be professional and cordial.

From all the advice given, this meeting is not a performance meeting; it is not a reconciliation meeting or let's have a chat and go another round - God forbid.

The decision is already made, they are gone. This one is not a firing, but a redundancy as the quickest way to exit them as advised by your legal team otherwise will take forever to get rid of them through a performance review that they will play you like a fiddle.

THIS IS AN EXIT STRATEGY.
THIS IS GOING TO BE GOOD FOR YOUR BUSINESS.
THIS WILL BE GOOD FOR YOUR TEAM MORALE.
THIS IS LONG OVERDUE.
THIS IS GOOD FOR YOU.
IT'S TIME YOU BOSSED UP!

Ensure you have a private room in your office to meet (not at all in view or earshot of others and not in a coffee shop where nosey parker from next door is there to spread gossip later on).

If possible, have tissues already in the room (do not carry them in with you) and ensure they are not on the main table but to one side or in a cupboard or drawer just in case they are required as it is likely to be an emotional time, especially if this soon to be ex-employee had no idea this was on the radar. And there is to be no judging if it is emotional.

Just be supportive to a degree, be nice and do not, I repeat, do not apologise, or say sorry. This is business!

Request to meet with the person.

Then follow all directions from your advisers, and here is an example structure and commentary, notwithstanding that you have already prepped with your legal team on how best to conduct the exit and follow their guidelines of the departure of this person.

[SAMPLE START]

Thank you for meeting with me today [name].

I have asked [trusted colleague] to be present with me for this meeting, and I will explain why.

Decisions have been made for the business, and with that comes changes on several levels, including that of staffing and personnel.

Therefore, in light of those necessary changes, today, your role is no longer, and as there is no other suitable role within the organisation, you are being made redundant from [company name], effective immediately.

Here is a letter explaining the redundancy payout, including any accrual of holiday pay and/or any other entitlements formalising your final payment as disclosed therein, which amounts to $ [specify dollar amount].

Any notice period required per your employment contract and/or stipulated by employment law (if applicable) has also been factored in and thus accounted for in the final payment.

You will not be required to work that notice period out; you will, of course, be paid for that time and you will be leaving us right now.

That final payment will be processed [state day and ensure it is completed promptly or as applicable per employment law].

DO NOT APOLOGISE.
DO NOT SAY SORRY.
THIS IS BUSINESS.
THIS IS NOT PERSONAL.

Do not make it personal regardless of how you feel, or how the person reacts, negatively or otherwise to you. You do not want to provoke nor provide any reason for them to have a case against you whether through an employment tribunal or fair work organisation depending on state and/or country that your company resides in.

Ensure they have their letter of redundancy.

If asked why me, why now and the tone and conversation are in some way soliciting why you have singled them out or picked on them, understand that it is natural for them to ask this.

State, as previously mentioned, decisions have been made for the business, and with that comes changes on several levels. This is one of them.

If the person has a moment, and we all do for a number of reasons, and this is a surprise to them for sure, then let them compose themselves with dignity.

Once that composure is regained or at least to a point where you assess time has been given to compose themselves, then say [name] it's time for you to leave now.

Stand and extend your hand to shake theirs and say thank you for their contribution. (whether you mean it or not, show that you do).

The standing and gesture to a handshake is the conclusion of the meeting. If not your style, then don't shake hands.

If applicable, then state, we will go back to your desk now so that you can gather your personal items.

Either you or your trusted colleague (who too must not say sorry whatsoever at any point) must walk back the person to their work area, office, workstation, etc. to collect their personal items.

Do not let them access the computer, touch equipment, etc. You must observe them all the way to exiting the premises.

If they are a genuinely nice person and based on how they conducted themselves in the exit meeting, let them briefly say goodbye to their immediate team only.

This is not necessary and only if you feel you can handle that situation, otherwise do not entertain it. There is always a possibility that this can get out of control with negative comments being made, so you take this route potentially at your peril or just be mindful of what you are getting yourself into. If it escalates then cut off any conversation, ask the team to move away, have the now ex-employee gather their belongings and finish this.

Escort them to the exit, say thank you, and I will ensure payroll processes your pay for you as we discussed.

[SAMPLE END]

DONE!
CONGRATULATIONS.
NEXT, INFORM THE TEAM WHAT HAS OCCURRED.
KEEP MORALE HIGH.
DO NOT TRASH THE PERSON.
STATE CHANGES HAD TO BE MADE.

Some will worry that there are more changes and people to be let go. That is natural to be concerned and if there are more to remove then do so immediately.

If there are no more immediate changes, then have a quick meeting to address the team on the change you made, in the best interest of the business and its mission. There are no negative comments shared on the now ex-employee, especially when they may have friends within the group and gossip later. You do not want any reason for all this to become undone or a continuing legal battle long after you think you have seen the last of them.

Once the team is communicated to, then have everyone return to work and monitor the team over the next few days to check everything is okay and no one else has started to play up.

Ensure that all access for the terminated employee is handled, redirected, passwords changed across all systems.

JUST GET IT DONE

When you finally move lazy people on the benefits are good, great, even fantastic on several levels:

✓ Your staff will sit up and pay attention that you don't take shit from anybody and passengers are not allowed.

✓ They may be relieved that this lazy you know what is removed from the workplace as they may have been carrying that persons' workload for who knows how long.

✓ It can go towards gaining some respect, possibly they may be concerned or worried, this so-called mid-life crisis moment of yours (which it isn't, but some may label it as such) means they are on your radar possibly, and so they really should take notice.

✓ You may observe a more concerted effort from the team or just in general, a change in the atmosphere, all going well towards a positive one.

✓ You personally may not enjoy the task of firing, cleaning the house, but you will feel much better that you stepped up and took action.

✓ It will also make you more direct with your hiring of new staff in that everyone goes on a probationary period regardless of the role and you have a very good contract in place that allows for dismissal should the candidate not be the right fit for the role. Right from the start if you sense any possibility that this person is a Lazy F@#K then exit them immediately.

✓ When other staff realise that you are creating a work environment that is just for that reason - work - and productivity is the key, to achieve the target, revenue and profit etc. then people who may have been a Lazy F@#K in hiding even change their ways or you just deal with them swiftly too.

Remember that you need to be thick-skinned in that you may be seen as harsh, a bulldozer, an asshole or any number of words people can come up with to describe you firing someone (albeit you are removing them not necessarily firing them in all cases), when in fact this is necessary to clean up the toxic within your workplace and keep the focus on what the company's mission is.

It sure as shit is not to carry dead weight passengers pulling a paycheck when they don't even pull their weight. All they have been doing is pulling your chain, and now after reading and studying this guide, that chain is going to ring the bell of ding dong you are gone.

BOOM BABY. FU!

BEST OF LUCK
WITH EVERYTHING

REMEMBER TO BOSS UP

HUMBLE FINAL WORDS

I know from personal experience and respect that you do too, that one's mental wellbeing is a personal and very unique way of handling your emotions, dealing with the stress that comes at you from all sides, the anxiety that builds up and the challenges that life seems to put in your way.

So, taking time out, that 'me time' even including support from others who care about you or are there for you, can help strengthen one's mental wellbeing.

It can help bring a positive outlook, lift your mood, help you deal with any difficult situations, take a new direction, and get the best out of life.

If you're feeling it, whatever 'it' is for you, then your family, friends and yes, most certainly your employees are feeling a version of 'it' also. And maybe it's just getting to understand them a little better, and they may need just a little help too.

It does not matter who you are. Pause for a moment and focus on positive wellbeing and get fired up.

YOU DESERVE NICE

www.ingramcontent.com/pod-product-compliance
Lightning Source LLC
Chambersburg PA
CBHW071528040426
42452CB00008B/927